LOOKING UP

Winner of the L. E. Phillabaum Poetry Award for 2022

Also by Dave Smith

DAVE SMITH

looking up

POEMS | 2010–2022

Louisiana State University Press Baton Rouge

Published by Louisiana State University Press
lsupress.org

Manufactured in the United States of America
First printing

DESIGNER: Michelle A. Neustrom
TYPEFACE: Bembo
PRINTER AND BINDER: Sheridan Books, Inc.

COVER IMAGE: *Emotional Tomatoes,* 1988, by Frank Cole.

LIBRARY OF CONGRESS CATALOGING-IN-PUBLICATION DATA
Names: Smith, Dave, 1942– author.
Title: Looking up : poems, 2010–2022 / Dave Smith.
Description: Baton Rouge : Louisiana State University Press, [2023]
Identifiers: LCCN 2022017770 (print) | LCCN 2022017771 (ebook) | ISBN
    978-0-8071-7852-2 (paperback) | ISBN 978-0-8071-7918-5 (cloth) | ISBN
    978-0-8071-7928-4 (pdf) | ISBN 978-0-8071-7927-7 (epub)
Subjects: LCGFT: Poetry.
Classification: LCC PS3569.M5173 L66 2022 (print) | LCC PS3569.M5173
    (ebook) | DDC 811/.54—dc23/eng/20220414
LC record available at https://lccn.loc.gov/2022017770
LC ebook record available at https://lccn.loc.gov/2022017771

For Dee

and for

Jeddie, Jed, Lael, Hunter, Bowden, Baird, Mary Catherine,
William, Boyd, and Lulu

Very simply he brings the clubhead around his shoulder into it. The sound
has a hollowness, a singleness he hasn't heard before. His arms force his
head up and his ball is hung way out, lunarly pale against the beautiful
black blue of storm clouds. His grandfather's color stretched dense across
the north. It recedes along a line straight as a ruler's edge. Stricken, sphere,
star, speck. It hesitates, and Rabbit thinks it will die, but he's fooled, for
the ball makes its hesitation the ground of a final leap: a kind of visible sob
takes a last bite of space before vanishing in falling. "That's *it!*" he cries . . .

—JOHN UPDIKE

                                            I cannot tell you
How beautiful the scene is, and a little terrible, then, when the crowded
    Fish
Know they are caught, and wildly beat from one wall to the other of their
    closing destiny the phosphorescent
Water to a pool of flame, each beautiful slender body sheeted with flame,
    like a live rocket
A comet's tail wake of clear yellow flame; while outside the narrowing
Floats and cordage of the net great sea-lions come up to watch, sighing in
    the dark; the vast walls of night
Stand erect to the stars.

—ROBINSON JEFFERS

CONTENTS

III.

IV.

ACKNOWLEDGMENTS

I am indebted to many who supported, directly and indirectly, the composition of my poems over fifty years. My thanks go especially to students for the life they helped me find in poetry. I am deeply grateful to the Virginia Commonwealth University Department of English, the Louisiana State University Department of English, the Writing Seminars at Johns Hopkins University, and the Creative Writing faculty of the English Department at the University of Mississippi.

Some of these poems first appeared in the following journals:

Aethleon: A Journal of Sports Literature: "A Sunday Story," "Bull Fight," "Rain Play," and "Thick Shell"; *Blackbird:* "Audubon's Peewees," "Breakable Jesus," "Developments," and "Reading Obituaries"; *Five Points:* "Blue Laws," "Dead Fish," "Dressing," "Louisiana Tree Frog," "Memorial," "New Neighbor," "Somebody's Jet," and "Uncle Melvin"; *Hot Rocks:* "Tomatoes"; *Kentucky Writers:* "The Secret of Herd Travel"; *Literary Imagination:* "February Fox," "Man Swimming in Home-Dug Pool," and "Now That I Am Dead;" *Literary Matters:* "Nobody's Dog"; *New Letters:* "The Room," "Silent Movies," and "The Thief of Small Toys"; *Shining Rock Poetry Anthology and Book Review:* "Flying in Sewanee" and "Lizards Running"; *Solstice:* "Two Poems about Love"; *Southern Quarterly:* "Quail;" and *Southwest Review:* "A Personal Baptism," "Christmas Memory," Club Legacy," and "Montana Bar Revisited."

LOOKING UP

City Point

. . . fossimo presi per incantamento
—DANTE

Dream spirit, muse I loved! Let me tell you
her skills, and how perfect her parts to me,
that red-mouthed, lank, straw-topped girl who
played me, witty as wind, heron sleek. Oiled
like lost gods, half-naked and lithe, we'd wheel
the salt waters in borrowed boats, skipping school,
to lie in the lonely cove past City Point,
blind to crabs eating the dead, so hot we boiled.

But it's always the same, isn't it, age, bloat,
decay's blisters and sores, tide-grinding fate?
In surf's silk we'd swim, then grip together,
lying how our love would go far in good boats.
What can it hurt to feel all again, to hear
love's tale of aches on dream's flesh-eating shore?

I.

Audubon's Peewees

I fixed a slight silver thread to the leg of each.
—J. J. AUDUBON

for Jeddie and Jed Smith

He sat with them until the baby birds took him
for one of them, his hairless hand
a mothering none resisted, the sighing
French hum of homesickness their ordinary
when he came, treats of worms, grubs,
a drop of goat milk for the dying one. Useless.

Silver threads, light as moon slip on night weeds,
they plucked and picked at until freed.
Life being a game, he attached them, then
dark-riddled, one by one, they removed themselves.
Blended into the nest, invisible but for eye-gleam,
all but one lost when winter drove them away.

Then, they return! Ice-morning, on his palm the male,
his female hovering back, juddering, cocked
peeps of fear, him squinting his blue eye.
His hat swallowed both, settling, as if in his brain.
A silver ribbon, ratty in the end, pennant.
What far flight! Hadn't they been everywhere together!

But where? A dream. With the moon sliding
past snow's patches old nests welcome.
Father oaks wailed in wind, monstruous shadows.
Dear little fellow, waking him, he would ask.
Half-closed, black eye blinking until it stopped.
What path? By what water? How to prepare?

The frayed silver flag it bore quickening,
the would-be artist leaned close.
And held his breath, and drew it so.

Witness David

Under ovals of buzzards sun keeps nudging,
I walk a narrowed fairway feeling lighter
as my body gives up weight, playing alone,
retired, mid–week, mid–summer, a traveler
in solitude the world requires, its last idea.
Where are the many, coming and going, some
by shades hidden, some unknown, who were,
salt and sour, the living who defined me?
And those above, patient in their hunger,
do they know me, David, who was once holy,
whose flesh women touched like a flower?
Their black shadows glide over me, unbroken
by light the Lord casts down as if not thinking
this stuff of all we are is worth everything.
Now mired in folly, wandering, I think how
creatures forced to approach and cherish only
the dead must find the image of wreckage
as the one truth never in doubt, they must
measure the axis and spool of change as all
life amounts to. But do they never turn back,
startled by love's face as it looks up blindly?
They do not speak, gathering factors of loss,
they hover beyond anticipation and regret
for the nothing hopeful, the nothing reborn,
presiding life's stewards, cleaning foul air.
David, I think of shouting up to them, David,
my cart full of clubs the golf gods gave me,
amused birds blacker than doom's dreams.
But I am not their target yet, just an outlier
thumping the ground to see what still lives,
harmless, they seem to agree, as I slump past
their companions musing in a maze of weeds,
my face burned red as the blood they smear on.

Red Throat

The hummingbird visiting my wife's roses
wears an old white halo of morning sun but
I see the iridescent dark of his truth. Now
he darts, self-redeeming, now withdraws,
hovers, reconsiders, then disappears into
newly dying blossoms. I feel my breath stop
as if I understand a meaning I did not see,
the way a writer listens even as words go
humming off in the brain. Oh bird, I think,
burst back into my light! Years pass like
a wink, then he casts his tiny whistle of joy,
commanding apostle, risen in a hairy pine.
Why have I never seen how he is hanging
so near, so patient, his hard eyes trued on
me? His body, beating, whispers: Tell me,
what you planted here, how good it tastes.

First School Day

My way went by fields hidden behind
trees, a house, path passing windows,
Scylla, Charybdis, or worse, the blind
flaming eyes that, if I bolted, might seize,

turn me to ash, then I never could go home.
I lugged my box, cheese sandwich, chalk,
pencil sharpened, tablet, and stone
from my own yard. I'd sling it if attacked,

or hold it if a giant wind came whirling.
Weeds rattled like sand and beach waves.
My walk could be more than a year. A bell
badgered my ears. I would not be saved.

But you called to me then, dream-smacked,
and taught me how to praise the dead
we revived in play-wars, rank on rank.
I was good with words, you with the gods.

How could I think you would die alone?
Face that told me I will be Achilles,
you be Patroclus, one heart, blood's one
unyielding gaze we'd have each for each.

"Always sing dreams, the best loudest."
Pretended toys, battles, foes come back now.
They speak of years redeemed from dust,
The life I love, words, path in, path out.

What's left to say? You'd hiss, "Everything!"
We yearned for big lives to choose, not rue.
Remember how we'd shit in their weeds?
When school ends where will I meet you?

Dressing

I was always good at cleaning dead animals,
something I learned to do to please my grandfather,
our morning's hunt done, him in his rocker.

Squirrels have hide as tough as Achilles, you can't
get a dull knife in that skin, so I taught myself
honing, sliding the stone to and fro until the edge

shone with my little-boy spit. Then at the ass
you slice up to the throat. The head slips off easy.
You collar-cut the legs, then grip and pull the fur.

Some little nicks here and there unslip the skin
if the creature wants not to give up its dress.
There's no formula for where to apply them, though.

Field dressing is a skill you will never forget even
if you haven't done it for years. I think of it now
and again, say when I see road-kill, a blotted mess.

The urge to be strict, efficient, certain comes back.
It's not rocket science, but time matters, prudence
helps prevent sickness or worse, you need to be able

to open up the bowels, dig out the waste, stomach
the rank smell of what's inside any animal, go
where the meat has a healthy, robust appearance.

It won't stay that way. You have to wash it now.
Preserve it with cool or salt or dry it out hard.
No matter what you do, it won't be a good taste

comes back when you see another dead body
on the asphalt but flare of the odor gushing out.
Like the worst moment on the toilet, new wife

lifting your head from your hands, all the dead
in the world seems to want to come out of you,
you can't push it back, and you can't forget it.

Prayer to a Tree I Loved

after Horace, Odes, ii.13

Tree of Heaven, strength of green, old heart shower me
    again with shade like a wise man's dream.
My neighbor feared you, he sent his dark crew with saws,
    chippers, a hauling truck. They hacked you
from sight, vanished leaf and limb. I curse the man's gods.

But can anger unrape us, can sorrow relimb us? What will
    rise from his poison he spreads all night
in our flowers like inexplicable evil? Cops we called said
    save your money, sleep on it. I want to kill
the man who killed you. Years ago I saw the KKK shriek.

They stood in my father's field, white sheets like shivers
    of flame up their pole-cross, words of hate
cindering the night furrows. In the morning a ghost ash
    drifted on our clothes, clotted and clumped
hung leaves, dog fur, the fixed face of a child with a doll.

Afterward, days did not change. We washed ourselves,
    stood alone with you. What could we do?
When we sang to beg Jesus for courage they sang with us.
    When we saw your wrens and finches cry
for saints, we were quiet. We need hearts hard as yours.

In my darkness I touch a piece of you, wood-god, silent as
    the face of Jesus, and I watch the man
who has killed you. I see house light flame his neck, cross
    his arms, back, trunk, until I feel the skin
blister, the ears tear like leaves, the spine snap. I pray now

to receive the peace of those who you held, the dreamers
      who lived here—shy owl and sly hawk,
ready to do what is to be done. Give me, oh Christ, that
      night-honed face a child has, looking up,
a wooden doll in her fist, head glowing with a kiss of flame.

Two Poems about Love

A DAY IN THE WOODS

Because a car careened after me, I fell in love
with the girl they gave me to escort one night.
Her boyfriend was crazy, so I asked her to tell me
answers to questions we went to the woods to ask.
Life is often more than the blackbird's flash of red
shoulders like strobe light, but sometimes it isn't.

I could see the bird go from pine branch to next branch
and you settled down on me, your skirt barely
covering your legs long and firm as a canoe paddle
we walked past going in. Held by your body, I saw
how a single bird could fly through my chest
more than fifty years ago. I want to say, Jesus Christ,

what happens when love comes in the open like that?
So much went on out of sight I couldn't stop
looking at grass bowers, boat houses, swamp rooms
no curtains keep, those places where legs part
to let in what feels like the flutter of a black wing.
You told me it was so. You said maybe it will go on

singing if we lie still, holding what we can, so we did.
After a while we forgot about the boy, the reasons
I was lying in the cool dirt, sun on splayed limbs.
I didn't think about birds much anymore, or say
what I heard crying there, black wings of
loneliness already in our mouths, sweet, sweet Jesus.

UNLIKELY STORY

Once I walked in a snowstorm for love
a woman had not promised me, but thought,
in truth, I could hear it calling. It wanted

no more than to live in my ear, dreaming.
Like an owl beside our bedroom, midnight,
all eyes in the top of the oak, unstopping
but enough pauses to make you listen.
That's why I was knee-deep, face iced,
no fear of the river hiding under the snow.
Now and again whips of wind on my skull
raked like off-angle dives of the talons.
Then that floating in soundless space you
feel is full of eyes watching, the tiny heart
of the moon suddenly bright like a body
where darkness flows. Men like to sing
to savor what they fear. The work of country
western music is devotion to the sickness
of hearts in such weather, tongues clotting,
ears blue-caked, breath like a fiddle's puff.
Best, we think, is remembering all in a bar,
whiskey, smoke, words thick with meaning
somebody's gouged in the wood, the names
all but hidden by varnish and dirt, a little
joke on the lips saying a man walked out
in a storm. He went into the raucous bar
where the woman was, who once loved him,
and then, then, etc., the end walks away.
Such pitiful music, so welcome, so often.
In Utah Mormons have a law no bars
within a mile of a school or church, but
bars, like legs, keep opening day and night.

Neighborhood Mechanic

A redwing blackbird waited for me pumping
up and down on the long blade of green,
his shrill strung-out hello full of the summers
of my boyhood, soon the smell of swamp
floated up, tide creeping where my legs hung.
He said you wouldn't believe all I remember,
so I threw a small stone at him, just as I had
years ago, and again he leaped in the air,
a black shine of feathers pirouetting, blood
on his shoulders like those who lowered Jesus.
I was waiting for my car, which was dying,
to roll from the old neighborhood mechanic's,
the day was late, the hot wandering of August
seemed to slow even the exquisite evidences
my witness looped for all to come near and see.
I could hear my mother's pans stir for supper,
tomatoes and onions bleeding, golden peaches,
newly sliced, I'd stolen from a neighbor's tree
these black wings had clung to like home,
the tree where I begged God she might not die.
I could see how my cost was going to be great,
the eyes that now and again flicked upon me
looked wet like new bearings, steeled without
scarring, or maybe the eyes of a martyr. Shrill
the sound of that breathing, and everything
glued to it like pieces of skin violently torn.
Terrible, I thought, the way innocence turns
in us, the way hope believes the worst has
moved on, the way one flick of small shoulders,
one edgy note trumpets all that you kept, all
you cast away for that small stone just waiting.

Louisiana Tree Frog

Deep summer night, black space like hung webs,
the dog has to go, so I go with him,
hand-light snapped on when I hear the one
waiting as if for me, a noise so outsized

for the tiny green body clinging to banana frond,
invisible splay of its grip as sure as Velcro,
skin so perfectly camouflaged nothing
can say how appetite springs, goes forward.

But it does. Oh Lord, the endless trilling
like a jackhammer in my head.
Once in a dream mania I rushed out
wanting to kill that shy fellow—he was

dying to call in his love, wanting, and hung
skidding and wallowing alone, one note.
My wife said, "You must be crazy."
There was no answer. I listened.

I had to imagine a tongue tasting darkness,
the slick that could catch any of us
catching only a dead-scented air.
I couldn't stand what it kept calling out.

I didn't know what it said, but I hated it.
In the morning, as in dreams, I knew
it would be gone. Amusing to her,
such a simple little pain. To me, pain

itself, gone. But only for a little while.

Blue Laws

In my town blue laws still cover everything,
so I take a walk out to the end of nowhere,
I pass the owner of a black Ford with a hood up
but he doesn't answer when I speak to him.
I pass a man leashed to a little white dog.
It's hard to tell which of them is wheezing,
so I say hello, but there is no answer. So,

I go down the hill where the magnolia blossoms,
white stars like a gunfight at sea, too far away
to hear, but explosions clear enough, the gods
trumpeting and chest-beating as is their way.
By now my arms are working up to a march,
lifting and falling, you can almost hear
Sousa come around the corner, the innocents

turning their heads, tired doves fluting away.
I'd like to enter a bar and put my fist down
around an iced draft beer, to protest the words
a blonde slim as a coat hanger spits freely.
I'd like to stay there into the blistered dusk,
maybe some fries, the door letting in exhaust.
Then I'd walk home, knowing you were there.

I'd really like that.

The Siamese

When Dee and I were just married we had
cats, Siamese, two howlers, sleek as clouds.
We must have wanted something small
and warm and even idyllic to hold nights
we sat flooding the room with TV's blue
glow, and we were discovering how little
you had to do for them, no letting them out,
not these princesses, no hose and yard bath,
no leash, no walks to christen our neighbors'
yards, no store bags for untimely deposits.
But nothing stays the same. One saw her
first mouse cross the apartment floor under
her belly, leaped up, jettisoned yellow pee,
as suddenly as if madness had come, and
left us, dying in her sleep, no explanation.
The other, suffering nightmares, hissed
herself awake, stalked curtains, attacked
me, then Dee, as we rolled to comfort
ourselves with dreams, music, even sex.
A kind lady who liked blue eyes laid
one fine meal at her door, she wagged her
whole rear end once, then gone like youth.
How often nights now I sit drinking in
guilts with my whiskey, sometimes seeing
those creatures move like my mother's
leopard coat, feline and fake, perfectly
licked to unfoul each blemish and chance
life offers. But how do we choose? Sound
they made in their passion hangs, is awful,
a tooth snapped in the mouth, but nothing
to what I feel when I remember my mother's
lies, men she trailed, her debts, the scorn
of screams from that pain–ridden believer.
Jesus will punish you, she spat, stiffening,
beauty in her bare, slow, mysterious breath.

Mother, let me feed you, I said, try to eat.
The same look on her face as those cats
crossing a new threshold, the door closed.
And, Jesus, that will to accept what's coming.

Some Horses I Remember

FIRST MARRIED

They circled us as we slept, our rented cottage just
yards from Bennet's Creek, tide we didn't know
rising where they liked to graze, salt air growing
thick as the storm breathed harder over us.
I woke and stood in a sleeping room's
lightlessness that was like hope waiting to be real.

At first it sounded like thumping in a dream, hooves
splashing water, belly of mare and foal
garlanded with foam, the buckskin stallion
leading, halting at the owner's shut gate
each time they came round, then pushing off
with shining shoulders. I saw some stand

alone in gowns of moonlight beneath fringy pines,
like gods, silent as blood spent, great heads
lifting in wind-bursts as if to speak.
I came from the bed of my bride
who dreamed above us like an angel.
They seemed to look up, as I looked to them,

lightning and dark, skies electric and blank,
those eyes like messengers. At the window
the rough pines were bending and touching,
weeping with rain, trunk and root real to me
in that decay of marsh, the slip-slip
of small waves beating ashore like boat hulls.

They wanted to go. They splashed, they stamped.
Then into the blindness of water, rain-lashed
ghosts, hearts in the boxed meadow we rented,
those pacing strangers, spattered, went,

every direction true and good and turned
from earth to a slickness of fish. Black took

hooves, black hurled horizons, black our ceiling,
black like the remembered we cannot save
or outswim, and now we had no house light
to pour over that ordinary yard, only a door
I flung open, shouting for what I hoped
could yet rise. But what can words do? Maybe

I did not see lightning scald those eyes but I saw
the flash lift from them like shield-sparks,
smoke on broad backs of the drowned ones.
All they tried to do was stand on what's
real, that was bottomless as hope,
unabiding as dirt nature hates and covets.

Tree limbs, gust-plunged, cracked like commands.
The storm shouted. Soon blackness only.
I shut the door, chose to dream, and climbed
to lie with a girl's love. Rain gentled the roof,
she opened to me. I did not then care
how horses swim against one another

but see now it seems so much desire cannot sink.
Mare and buckskin stayed up longest
like gods we must ride until we ride ourselves.
Even so before them the foal rolling away,
white eyes like moons they had stared after.
Then water shrinks, then so many days of stink.

OLD NAG VISITED

Blotched swayback in a local paddock
drifts from one side to the next, is
palsied, pocks turf. Acts like he sees

what is coming, distant as dark. Waits.
Then seizure works him rib to ass,
blows up crusted nostrils, snorts, farts,
eyes, oil-slick, roll as if at death, legs,
for Christ's sake, all but dancing. Air
gives him no way but rage, a brute's

history we do not know but can see
in lumped muscles, nerves making
fists under hide. Bones zipper
scars boy riders left like graffiti,
his past of welts, wens, growths.
All day he stands, stone, but it comes,
whatever he keeps, then hooves go
after stallions, or stars, or jeering gods.
No one can say anything true of him.

Entering like little priests sparrows
quietly ask why he hasn't been killed.
They step and scour the divoted spine,
prayers needling and eating. He rips
himself raw as they dance. Sex purse
hangs, sways, mudded. Cruelty lights
his winter day, his lathering foam
seems the same madness Vietnam
soldiers cast once home. We wonder
is this the hell at the end of days?

But sometimes beauty inexplicably
lifts him, pure high-step and side-slide
seems routine, the gods triggering
a boy inside so he prances and huffs
until his muzzle hangs. But watch out,
something will tell him kick the shit
out of everything, and he tries. Or he's
down, rolling, piss sprayed. Let him
die, some say, his pain untranslatable.

But we don't. We just keep coming.
He'll drink our beer, eat a cigarette.
Death doesn't seem to want his kind,
or is amused how he hurts himself.
What's stranger than life is the bite
of horseflies he wears with no sound.
We don't want to know what's felt.
We're with you pal, we shout, hoping
the next beer makes him explode. Ok,
it's how sickness works. Sometimes.

IF YOU WERE A HORSE

Who are we alone? A basketball
still, night bugs. My TV news on.
Thirteen, nameless, a boy points
a gun at a brother who mouths off,
ten, so under the hoop life pieces
blow sticky in darkness like flies
bumping a kitchen window. Inside,
the mother files her nails, love's
music gallops down the hall.
The hand leaps, a horse's tongue,
wildly alert, tasting terror's world.

I look in his eyes, as my mother did.
I was his age, thief, crying my truth.
Let it go, she said. I say it for him.
He hears everything. His mouth
tries to say *Please* to lift the body.
Me too, Christ, but it's just drool,
just blood and nerve, vomit and piss,
the animal in us scared. If he was
a horse what words would calm
where the deep thuds in his chest?
Moonlight wails I hate you forever!

Can't you see him circle, all-eye,
Mike's dream shirt bloody, split
shoes, gold chain pulling down
the hoodied head that bucks at air
where lightning is? The truth is now
nothing will be real again. See,
hope's frantic panic says I have
to be a boy, thirteen, all I am.
So we will be you, my tongue lies.
If you were a horse, who wouldn't
hold you? So you wouldn't vanish?

Febuary Fox

Oxford, Mississippi

Awake at dawn I stand before iced glass.
A flap of newspaper the night's left limp
clings to a pine sapling, even big words
bled out like poor women stabbed or shot
in Memphis, where TV hurls at us now
the awful, ordinary assaults we escape.
Soon, I'll eat, dress, start my car for work.

Strutting on nail-tips a gray fox glides past,
fur chrystalled in a razory sunlight
that glints, a halo on his rippling moves.
His black nose is hooked on a scent
like a hunger. Each step thinks of the lift
of her tail like a stripper's boa, never why
he's here, as I am, the fragment of a dream.

Once or twice we've heard females scream.
Sometimes my dog's pen reeks of spray
sudden as a glance in a bar, the stink
of furtive law he lets us keep to, who asks
no one what days mean, or why stars
raise our faces, or what we'd give to move
as he does, toward her, on earth that steams.

Flying in Sewanee

Once in Sewanee, Tennessee, I went outside
naked, a fully-grown man. It was foggy
up on the mountain so no one could see.
Inside me my blood sugar had plunged so
I believed I could fly, I guttered my arms
up and down, I made noise like a heron's
deep in my throat, I pushed the grass to lift
my fatness into the silver air. It took time
but I remember how the deep offside of
the mountain called me like a waterfall
a child might tumble into. By then Dee was
tugging my arm, afraid, trying to anchor me,
her voice that shrill whistle of the red-wing
when she grips the marsh-grass flutter-top.
Some would believe I never flew up at all,
saying it was only the nakedness of an idea
that makes a man confuse what is true. But
I remember every detail, starting with a door
opening, birds I couldn't see in morning fog,
voices of people on the golf course nearby,
the brush of cool pine needles on my chest,
my feet landing on crowns of moss, then
her face with its flame of anger, an angel's
grimace when a demon has grabbed her parts.
I have heard they cannot be captured but
sometimes the right lie will work to bring
forth the love that seems like hurt in a saint.
I can't think of anything else to explain how
often, over more than fifty years married,
I have gone flying and she brought me back.
Surely that is the proof, even if no one else
saw her struggle to stay on the ground, of
how love has kept us flying, up and down,
up and down, body to body alive. For now.

Uncle Melvin

He wasn't my uncle, it was only a name,
but they gave me to him for the day,
so we plunked our lines in the fast water
of the Potomac, I found myself far enough
from his old man's gaze, I could be
free, or what freedom feels like to a boy
only nine, only held to the world
by bare feet, a body light enough to fly.

It must have seemed to me I was flying,
his light pole casting itself loose,
my hand's opening flinging all I ever was
afterward, not even a quick shadow
yet with all the current's shades
reaching and splashing like the uncaught
hands I did not know how to grasp.
That's how it is, you are dropped in quick,

no matter what you have done, no love
enough to save you whatever they say.
The bank mud knows to be slick,
birds whip in sunlight like frantic words,
what's in the flow keeps on going.
I remember looking up at blurry sky,
then a limb hung low, grabbing it,
knowing now I knew as much as he did.

A month on he lay in the wooden box, face
the same as that floating on the water
where his line was gently tugged by something.
The others shoaled around him, sisters,
brothers, from the same net of flesh.
When they mumbled about his poor soul
I imagined it flying out, then into the deep
flow, maybe catching a branch, maybe not.

Nobody's Dog

Three boys with little to do, one older, and bigger,
down in the innards of a house somebody builds,
but not today, shade cool like the big woods, the dog
nobody's got a name for hanging with them, tail
wagging when they come near. The faint clean
odor of Georgia pine ripped rises everywhere
they settle, and move, and settle again.
Then one pulls it out, his motion
like waving off a fly, their talk pushy, jeering.
Then silence, creak of the unfinished
rafters naked around them. One
will remember the razoring slants
light drives down upon them like bright nails,
another keeps the dog's watery gaze
that will always seem to him like a hunger
nobody ever gets filled, and the third—you see him
rise now, the thing in his hand, then kneeling
at the last, the stupid grin like the soldier
gripping the dirty lance where Jesus is
only meat that will shudder and give way.
Nobody knew this was about to happen. No one
of them waking in the summer smell and the human,
uncertain what day would bring would have come
imagining this, not down those raw stairs.
Better to steal from your mother,
better to strike your sister with a nailed limb,
better to dive under a half-sunk boat, accidentally
raking your head on the keel, barely
enough breath to stay alive, and better to keep
your mouth shut. Better never to kneel after
the one who holds the whining dog,
never to look at the face which looks like a piece
of wood torn under the skin, and never
to remember the ease, the day ending, the words
practiced on the walk home, saying them

as if into the mother's ear, you were not anywhere
today, not with anybody, there is no story
that could be told and now you are hungry. So
in the tongue-and-groove pine-paneled kitchen,
dog-colored like dusk. Her singing. Bacon shriveled.

Golden Curls

How hard holding a single truth is reminds
me of the problem of Jesus you couldn't lose
anywhere you looked in my town. His face
in the gas station next to the Baptist Church,
golden curls like wood shavings spooled
his shoulders on Bob's Barbershop calendar.
It was always December, him alone. Except
where Marilyn Monroe hung up with him,
pure, perfect tits, beside the five-sleeve rubber
machine in Casteen's Pure Oil men's room.
Dirty light gave his blue eyes a smeared look.
Maybe it was the greasy touch of fingers.
Maybe town boys coming in there had a use
for a martyr, a saint, a steady looking-at each
must have got for every quarter plunked in.
I'd ride to church with friends, walk over,
say Hi to old boys, anxious as hell, wash up,
then on to Sunday school across the street,
fresh gum in mouth. I wouldn't sing funny
or screw up my face as they did mocking me,
no matter they said I couldn't be half as good
as a queer or a black girl. I promised Jesus
I wouldn't slip in dirty words the hymns
didn't say like the old boys did, I wouldn't
let my head's eyes roll like Little Richard's
or grease my hair like Elvis. But still I went.
I needed to see what went on over there,
Mr. Casteen screaming they better get right,
clean the place up, for Christ's sake, stop
fucking around or, boom, there'd be trouble.
So I'd go back, make bad promises, be happy
to sit with ladies who fanned the perfumed air
over the face of Jesus. He was everywhere,
one body watching the others come, and love's

gaze not stopping anyone it saw, even though
all you had to do was nod to the golden curls
and not believe he wasn't ever Him, same as
the sorry men, looking up, washing the hands.

A Personal Baptism

I sit inside a wall of hydrangeas, pale heads
jostling against the glass, the thunderstorm
touching the world with its first soft gusts.
The ancients understood what was meant
by the oncoming growl of thunder, steps
hurling down corridors of the gods' houses.
They're coming, a brain must have screamed.
So I hunch up as men and women once did,
facing distant dark clouds, words scrambling
like the wrens and finches trying to hold on
where soon rain will knock them to the dirt.
Try to pray, son, the preacher whispered, but
prayer was for something wanted, I'd learned,
not for telling the gods to go fuck themselves
for driving off a good day, scaring the fish
in our pond, sending the old dog under the bed.
It wouldn't be them to clean up his messes.
I looked into the preacher's face, into nostrils
flaring like the monstrous gills of the gods,
expecting what? I was only a boy, his hand
pushed down to seal off my mouth and nose,
and then I was inside the holy pool looking
at the face twist and grow horns of water.
I could see a tongue move, but no sound
and it seemed like a long time, and I wanted
to say the right words badly, to be lifted up.
Then it happened, the cheering like thunder
in our church, water hurled away from me,
preacher barking out my redemption's work.
In the vestibule elders, gatekeeping wizards
with long, leathery fingers shook my hand,
no miracle at all, and I was to them nothing
but routine. The way the world is when I try
to pray, eyes closed, hoping if I open up

I'll own their red eyes, scaled skin, my steps
suction-firm, my slow hiss of words too ugly
for gods to understand, much less to forgive.
What else is there to the story of belonging?

Dead Fish

after Horace, Odes, i.6

Sometimes in late afternoon I wonder why
I go on writing about banged-up boats,
marshes where east wind drags a sour stink,
men's sewage sliming the gold-tinted spears
you'd be hard pressed to imagine as glory,
a word rank in the mouth as saltwater bilge
I've swallowed and floated happily on.

Men go out in sinking boats, nets halo forth,
wretched catches of fish, small thrashing lives
come boiling in, hand over hand. This isn't
courage or honor, only hunger's push.
Not heroes, they trundle rattly trucks home,
they beat their children, they guzzle beer
until they fall like dung, damp rag piles.

They don't dream of Ulysses warring with fate.
In my own service days I only once faced
the face of a general. I forget his name.
On TV men like him praise the new killing,
terrorists with grants, social programs, drones.
They carry iPads. They wear cheap suits.
I wonder what labors, what evils they've known.

Then I write of horses my love and I loved,
dogs we thought would never die, houses,
kitchens a friend could stand drinking in next
to a wheezing neighbor who reeked of fish
he's offered because, he says, he caught them.
Sometimes I think I ought to be more serious.
Then I write about what I can remember

when the bed accepts me and I feel the weight
of myself sinking more and more. My love
beside me breathing harder, the moon is
filling our house with pleasure like seafoam
silvering the marsh edge. The tide is going,
wind in the trees makes note of it, lying
alone we can feel death in all things slink away.

Cow Story

Why I want to tell this story, if it is a story,
puzzles me the way philosophy does,
it's not of any actual use, you can't apply
a moral instruction, no one benefits,
the best thing to be said is it entertains
if, sitting on a burgundy leather couch,
you feel your mind drift back to a moment
when you thought you understood what
had happened, why the day after would be
inevitable and vicious in its lovely pain.
But that had no more logic than this story,
which isn't a story, now that I think of it.
It's only that Dee and I were early in love,
we liked hearing Jimmy Moore's cows moo
two, three fences away, wanting to come in,
be counted, get fed, waiting seemed too long,
so one might lift his heavy neck, his number
in his nose his only name, and just bellow.
The next one, darker but almost a twin,
thought the issue required clarification, so
his comment lifted over the loblolly pines,
and soon the herd was a legislature facing
an issue not one could define or remember.
Dee liked wine but I'd take a Pabst, we'd
sit by the river smelling salt, the voices
of other humans beyond the dark surface
sounding almost our parents calling us in.
But we were married now, feeling ambition
drove us to comment. But it wasn't that,
really, it was only love making us want
to speak to anything of how we felt. So
I'd lift my mouth, open wide, and let go
the best moo I had. I've seen them waddle
to the fence, watch me to see what I had
to say, one or two's answer soft as words.

Long nights, touching, we'd lay in bed
working out ideas, visions, our future.
Even now, when I feel bullish, I'll give one.
Our grown children like to say "oh Dad,"
as if nonsense has no value to a society.
That's why my wife likes to sneak me a kiss,
one filled with discussions, talk, and sighs.
Her certainty I can do it again understood.

A Tasteless Revelation

My mother said, staring at her bright, new nails,
"You've been to college but you're ignorant."
It hurt me to hear that truth, I wanted to know
why a man I admired was found like a boot
in his yard, and no one seemed to care. Sunday

home for lunch I said what happened to our Rich?
I can still see how she set down the dish of stew
and bread on the back porch for her black man,
eighty or more, him eating fast, then the raking,
then I'd drive him home. He'd whistle if he saw

a girl, the smell on him like old leaves. Up, down
he scraped, planted, pretending never to see us,
his scheme no more to us than why leaves fall.
"There must be somebody else, there always is,"
said my mother bent over hydrangeas he'd put in,

stirring her drink with her finger. I half-listened
as I used to do trying to write, hearing that rake
pick into dirt, then stop, then slowly start again.
Our faces hung blank as pew plates. I teased,
"What does Jesus want? "Well, a good yard man

is hard to find." She *was* funny. With two loved
ladies my afternoon flew by like that dead man
his old wife pitched out the window, then cried.
Things happen, mother said. He wasn't like us.
Grandmother nodded as if answering a question.

The Golden Mean

after Horace, *Odes,* ii.10

Dear Friend, I'm reading Horace on heroes.
The truth is I'm astonished to find him boost
the golden mean as the true path. It's trivial
grab-your-balls last-gasp urging that works,
human change is hard, preacher-talk is lard.
My high-school line coach taught Latin
as life lessons, his life a twisted sentence.
He bloodied us all August until the last boy
gagged, a fair angel he made fit for dying.

Isn't it heroic to suffer enough to win once?
We lost routinely. He'd never played, books,
dreams his only passion, so it seemed. Pale
as a yeast roll, one day caught, his fat hand
down a running back's jock, oh how he cried
I'm no hero, Father. But less saintly dads
summoned the fires of hell. He fled. Entered
on tip-toe guilt's exile, tried penance, hailed
redemption, prunes, visions, odes by Horace.

But we are what we are. Our outpost burg,
wanting giants made of its losers, hired him
to finger-poke truth, turn boys to men, push
us past the drool of gods and the nightmares
of dead heroes in poems. You want to be me?
He called us fags, girls with dicks, and beat us.
We gaped like rabid dogs. He got canned.
Fall 1960 we crushed the Wilson Presidents.
I'd hug that bastard hard to do it one more time.

Club Legacy

When a car killed my father, my ex-Petty Officer
uncle hung around, wanting to talk. I wished
he would go home, back to selling dishwashers,
his puffy face beaming at housewives lusting
for Kenmore machines. After a while, he did that.

Then I noticed my father's golf clubs were gone,
a dinged-up but friendly-sized set I asked for.
My mother, decades before I came along,
wiped her baby brother's brow in sickness,
promised him anything he might want, only just

live, she whispered. So he did it, his con's grin
full of whatever you wanted, good or bad,
his bright even teeth enough to sell rust
even to my mother. A totaled Thunderbird.
Great deal, he said, new title, almost a new car.

Vanished, those cheap Sears clubs, and the wrists
and fingers of war vets who tried to hack out
failure's hero shot, death wedge or bullet
cracked five-iron. Weekends, out they went,
deep in weeds, beer after beer, trying to be better.

"Take them," she said, in despair, no answer
where anything was, why death drove off
with my father, why lumps swelled my uncle's
belly, why the days would leave her in bed
gagging "Why me?" All you can do is to dig

past moldy suitcases, the blue of rotted uniforms,
unpack what years layer and leave, a handful
of shafts I unbent and steel-wooled to gleam
like my father home from a war, that love
crying when I asked. "They're gone, just gone."

The given can't be kept, the kept can't be given.
You look like both of them, she liked to say.
Men I barely knew. But maybe the truth is
like balls they hit. When I swing those clubs
I imagine it's how they looked trying to get better.

The Room

Last night in my dream you were alive again, the look
on you still, skin like runneled mud, and you spoke—
I can't remember what you said—I knew it was you.
The table's clatter of eaters, voices rising the way
love plays together. They weren't sad at all, drinking,
as if your death was one fine thing to celebrate.
I could see you were dead though you greeted me,
you told the same joke, a man enters a bar, we laughed.
I was sure I understood everything. Toward the end I saw

they were dead, too, and I began to sob, really tolling out
tears, breath vanishing, the way I had decades ago.
What happened to us father? Wasn't there a moment
your car rolled? I put my hand on the hearse, that
oniony smell of Spring dirt rose. In this dream
a girl I had been in love with smiled, her blood-red
mouth the one Marilyn Monroe had, only teeth
brown as your shoes they brought me in a bag, gold
Masonic ring, a shirt with your smell. I was seventeen.

The girl stood by me as you lowered into the clay hole.
I planted their boxwoods, served church suppers,
Sunday School friends said the girl I loved was
better in the dark than Monroe. They said rise up,
boy, make a profession of faith. I did and I saw
no life stayed pure, or saved. Just what happens.
I want to understand your joke, the girl I dreamed,
those faces grotesque with joy, passionate years
of talk in corners over sausage and beer, and that room.

Black Ice

Baltimore

How can you believe what you can't see?
Jesus said believe in me to Peter, and to others,
and they didn't blink, they gulped and swallowed
maybe, but no doubt what was belief then,
the way a nausea drools, then convulses you.

In Baltimore it spread because a host of
weathers comes together and the days are black
in their mood, hurt's just waiting, you are not
anyone special, not chosen, but you believe
in yourself words you hear rasped as you pass

an alley, maybe late for lunch, or leaving church,
or like me, opening the mailbox, just a little
step, no trouble expected, and the whole of you's
flying, a failed physics assumption. Only
even that doesn't last, there's a superior premise

under the invisible, and it's harder. I dumped
like a horse I saw a girl strike with a two-by-four.
Half under my car, freezing, I started to pray.
Let me get up, please. I sounded like a boy
years ago in the dark practicing for Jesus, or

at least hoping I would sound real to the faces
when I professed my faith. After a while
I crawled to a bench, a perfect afternoon empty
as my heart, no cars, no walkers, how could I
not see how slippery the world was, and wait?

II.

Call and Response

Out of sleep's fog I finally floated up, fumbled
phone from bedside table, on knees in darkness fell,
felt under bed the ringing call hello
thick voice southern black
looking up taking time to be sure
I was the one wanted, so I proved I was me,
birth date social full name loud
bumping things where she waited hello
yore momma went unresponsive
but what could such words mean now
sun not up yet, my mother in her room at the home
beepers on, lights flashing then I could see
the merciful red glow ambulance backing, her
small body hauled up, lacy nightgown
("What a *woman* wears!")
puckered immodestly, flabby legs, hurry
siren she wouldn't hear driving, brown steady gaze
I'd always known, she'd spend hours trying
to tell which road she'd taken, mind
desperate for familiar mailbox, yard light, bad curve
where tires howled if you drove too fast.
I often did. She could yank me alert as a dog.
Still on my knees I heard the woman
breathing she went unresponsive
flat air toneless wait then asked I say
back name numbers as if she's afraid
to lose me, connection words cracked up maybe
something more wrong her not knowing
who I am how bad I am. Old man
sitting on the floor alone looking up crying
for hands to lift, faint drift of sea
smell where she once held me and the tide turned.

Developments

I told my daughter I would pay for the life
of a child she and her husband couldn't.
I said think of it as a loan, a kind of faith
I once felt before my life brought mistakes.
I knew it was to help me believe in love.
I have always loved this daughter and I have
enough money for food, whiskey, golf, so
why not? Nobody lives forever, we agreed.
Then Lulu arrived, and good days, markets
up, house holding on better than expected,
Dee's broken eye not too bad, insurance
for my blood sugar gone crazy, my elbow
needing a new nerve, my neck suffering
what doctors called old-man loss, all of it
a tale of what's coming soon. I think, So?
Then I see a child alone on a street. I think
Christ, what will happen to love when I go?
In the brutal sun of the golf course I stand
waiting my turn and stare at the limp trees,
as if they know something. Beyond them,
bulldozers, backhoes, bobcats scrape at
roots where soil stinks in high sun, voices
of men on roofs call out in giddy Spanish
as if celebrating the solemn dance of death.
Soon enough it will be quiet as a cemetery.
I think how they must be making up tales,
as gods do, each hammered laugh some
new view of sand trap, green, ball banged
out of bounds, briars where big snakes lie,
the bad shots, the bets we will curse. Jesus,
as if life's only this play of words in the air.

The Least

This year's mallard survivors, not yet fully
colored, sleep like two dead lumps in grass.
What's happened to the hen huddling them
this Spring, leading her bobbers on the pond?
Gone now, the noisy drake with his issued
commands, a boorish glider strictly followed
even by big-nose turtles who get everything.
Only two of the original dozen, that happy
signature on the water, rise to greet us when
we open the porch door, holding Cheerios
because we are gods to them, their mouths
cry praise for our impressive generosity. But
sometimes we wave them away, silent, for
we did not make them, we do not benefit
whether they come or go. As fate pleases.
Yet how hard to resist desire to redeem each
creature from the murk of its invisible past.
We walk them to the dark shudder, we snow
our gold Os and the pond splits and wrinkles,
the deep turns snout-up, grass silently stands.
We imagine they feel a part of what we feel,
though the heads sway in the sun as if empty.
Don't they, through naked feet, know the least
insuck or exhale that moves over the bottom?
In the top of the cypress a white crescent
ticks his head less than an inch, ordering our
witness to go on, and then a storm starts, soon
big gods throwing up bodies, flooding earth
with their hurricanes of piss because we do
not love the inexplicable answers they give.
Today there was no bell, siren, bang, or voice.
Lords, we said, our hands hang like featherless
wings, but let us fan you in our tribute of wheat.

The Happiness of Women

Happiness has no measurable pace.
—R. P. WARREN

In late sun I walk to the pond and this season's ducks.
They've come far, like the sound of happiness, now
they shove their feathery bums up, they vacuum
the gummy bottom, dislodging what stinks and keeps
on daily dying, layering itself under matting leaves
like a book's untouched pages. The mallard hens
have so little time, and much to enact, moss-backed
turtles rising, heavy clouds, the big geese barging by.
Still, like new mothers gathered in grassy yards,
they seem to celebrate and they hang upside down,
heads sorting out the rankest matters, fish idling close
for what's set free, and new flights churn the water
brown as old blood. They come and go like Baptist
ladies who taught me never to forget Jesus loves
a good laugh. I remember the eyes always winking,
awake in hallelujahs. And the noise that wasn't just
happiness, but somehow a brute acceptance of drakes,
the hold-down's gasp and swallow before the burst
finally into light. Some can't live, they die floating,
beaten, parts pulled into the mud. Soon frogs bellow.
So I remember the bonneted women at Easter when
I was a boy, each one outrageous in her promise of
redemption, her colors and wobbly big-flower hats,
bobbling our names. I knew they could inhale all
the death night might bring, and sing all Sunday,
and fill our tables with all we'd need. Like blossoms
their bodies drew us to them, lacy breasts buzzing.
But arms would still go slack in a far room. But
now the pond's light makes a face glint, like joy,
its mouth purses to speak, but is dry, and is nothing.

It remembers me, I am sure. It wants to kiss me with
all it has believed. It has makeup on bruises of blue.
I know it wants to ease my fears. Its breath struggles
like happiness, feet move, words drift off in bubbles.

A Bargain for a Boat

My granddaughter Lulu recoils at the noise
of motors, mowers, hedge cutters, the usual
assaults in the neighborhood, her small face
coils like a swatted wasp, she glances past
my comfort like the fox sprinting to a tunnel
under our groomed azaleas. Still only three,
she scrunches in my arms and tries to hide
from everything time is hurling against her.
But there's a little boat gliding over the pond—
she wants down, she wants to run to catch it,
I have to hold her back, so now tears come.
I feel the warm moisture on my cheek, I feel
the old gravity of sorrow. We stand together
as the world roars and I remember the face
of my mother on the mortuary's gurney, calm,
as if she has just wakened, and the way earlier
she told me she once dreamed she was destined
to scream all her life, and never know why. I
bent my rough cheek to whisper help, as now I
tell Lulu the boat will come for her one morning.
One way or another, that much has to be true,
even if the air shudders in terror as my mother
said it did during the World War when I came
alive into her arms. Maybe Lulu believes me,
maybe the gods have not whispered in her ears,
who appear with their bags of grins, flashes
of joy, for a peaceful acceptance slowly goes
everywhere Lulu looks. Bargain for it, elders
said, promise them whatever they want. So now
in my head bent over the pond I imagine how
I promise not to gut their babies, pour motor oil
past lips, nail hands, no poison ivy or fire ants.
Gods, I say, let's make a deal. I keep my wrath,
you keep morning a still boat on a slick pond.
Like my mother's face, a rock against my kiss.

Thick-Shell

Thick-shell, the size of a man's head.
I found him crossing the 6th fairway,
beyond the dogleg I couldn't navigate.
He'd made his way over the wicked
slope that ricochets many a good stroke
into water so deep the bottom is secret.
He was headed toward a tree-line shade.
But it would be night before he'd plow
that nose under ages of aromas, leaves
like memories, the tiny tongue licked
out to taste whatever welcomed him.
Being old now, I'd seen him before,
or one like him, so I wasn't astonished
at the pond-web on his back, growths
like stars on a ceremonial coat. I wanted
to wait in homage until he had passed,
even though sun felt like death coming,
so I stood swinging my club, practice
it would seem to my companions urgent
to get ahead. Before long I heard myself
whisper there was little time left. Was I
wrong to think I saw the bony head lift
as if sighting some ancient tree or rock
he had dreamed in pond-muck, as if now
the words I said seemed the god-voice
of a son he might depend on and hie to?
The pond past the dogleg steamed like
a devil breathed to blind my best shot.
Because I watched him, I knew I could go
the way this thick-shell did. I would dream
deep woods past the green. He was there
already. I heard something making salute
like a tree of goldfinches. Or old fathers.
It was where you don't want to land and wait
or practice until they call, when it's urgent.

Armadillo

My dog once chewed up the ass of one trying
to transcend our backyard fence, our tomatoes
saved, the dog bloodied. But the corpse was gone
next day, no shroud of bone or flesh left behind,
the sort of thing that gives rise to legends, myths
of redemption, lies of visitation. They aren't
native here but they survive wherever fate sends
them, leathery skull-cap suits they wear enough
to make people call them evil and turn noses
away when the evidence is heaped. They don't
make any more noise than people who scream
at the occasional one head-down in a garden, but
the shuffling click of toenails, the breath-whisper
when the TV goes off, the dog pads out, that's it.
The rumor is they've been bringing us disease
for years but unseen, they keep to themselves,
they don't ask much, they don't attack, they eat
what they find, then move on like angels, slow
as night drags out the warm stillness we dream in.
But they are sure as hell no angels, more like
immigrants. Bodies mashed by the roads, tiny
tarry mouths, stained by wood, produce, garbage.
What language do we have to understand them,
all those clicks and grunts and gasps in the dirt?
I felt sorry for my dog, he looked ashamed maybe
he knew he killed an angel, a big one creeping
near the tree he liked to pee on. I asked him what
the creature said but whine, whine was all I got.
Tomorrow, I said tersely, we'll go look for his ass.
I knew we wouldn't find him, we'd flash lights
and swat palmettos and wave nooses and ropes
like searchers long past. It would just get dark,
we'd go home to snacks, calm as bearded gods,
cold beer, pigs' knuckles. Lies about evil or worse.

Yellow-Headed Night Heron

He wasn't born good, or even much loved,
this outcast tiptoeing our wood fence top,
legs a dwarf midshipman's seeking stillness,
his buzz-cut feather top knotted in wind as
his needle-beak compasses and scans. Out
in the road cars whizz. What can he want,
his scruples leaving him on that last post?
We've known for weeks a plan hatched
high in the live oak left driveway and grass
silvered with the littlest gulpers flying
from something's mouth like bitter secrets.
So he must have been up there with parents
who believed him the best they'd ever do.
I mow over the skeletal anchovies crisped
and soundless as terror he must have felt
when the parents left, like my father who
vanished one Sunday morning in May.
Of course, he'd have to climb down, all
of him an ugly edge, a gape they gave him,
dusk to dawn, all he had for his guide-go,
but maybe enough for Louisiana after all,
to rise from thorns, poisoned fields, ponds
acid-dried, trees hacked for new suburbs.
I feel myself rooting for him, feet saddled
with big claws, a lump with flight wings
stuck in his back, come-along of his jaw
making a sort of Morse code burp. Where
is such a misfit to live but here? I imagine
such couplings must be outsiders, partners
stepping off, not our kind, legally invisibles.
They live out there where fish don't fly.
They bring them to us like nightmares of
longing, these small ones waiting, gripped
just over the violent world we can't explain.
They hang around, vanish. They don't explain.

Somebody's Jet

Today I write about a fuselage, body
a bird's idea, USAF on its long nose,
a canopy of pines, all intact (Guns?
Flaps? Digital gauges?). Now anchored
to black earth. What history explains
the unexpected survivor that belongs
nowhere exactly? Beside I-55 outside
McComb, Mississippi, tendoned
to earth as if by the gods, a cockpit
of blue sky, so I pull over. I see
the squadrons, tearing pop-pop-pop.
Maybe someone came home to die
but got a good deal on an old plane.
Why not? No sign, no school, no brick
monument in sight. No people look up
shy at such power, but small trash says
someone dreamed truth here. Who?
I've stopped before, stood in wild grass,
watched a three-legged dog. He wasn't
fast enough. Gray fur, tufts, whiffed.
Nothing more American, briar woods,
fence unseen, broken bricks, foundation
gone, leaf-cupped rain. Little cross
flower-painted, pale ghost bicycle.
Name weathered out. A light wind
scratches from the road, so I think
of a young man's gaze, the brilliant
fury of firing lights. How alone
one can feel in the moment the act
takes up the body and leaves the shell
you were, inexplicable, the rest of it
like that dog gone on, somewhere
licking itself, or chewing so intently.
Not meaning anything, nobody's
answer, just what happens, here, now.

Butterfly Bush

This morning sunlight clear as Fall croakers,
humidity vanished, the storm, like God's breath,
sending fogs, mists, gray scuds piling past wharves,
masts, the heat-sweated shore of our tidal inlet.

Now the butterfly bush offers purple-blue
cones, thick miniature growth on the exhausted
skeleton summer's drought had almost denuded.
Who could have expected such late blossom?

Carefully, delighted, I thumb water to a spray.
Soon you will wake and call me to bed.
A new poem's first lines hover, a butterfly
slides close. My feet are naked, dirty, and wet.

Montana Bar Revisited

in memorium Richard Hugo

All those poems fishing knee-deep in trout wily as gods
and last-stop bars he loved falling down. The dead gathered
there, knuckles ripped, beer mugs, whiskey floats, sprawl
of the knocked-over, the slurred, the missed, those scabs
on doors, rust-buckets outside. He wanted to tell you
more than he knew, at the table that redhaired beauty
scratching on her pad what you ought to want. He would
remember no cold she couldn't heat up. He liked that kind
of tale, the solitaries in a sick house, a blistered bannister,

a busted Buick's thump and belt-whine, a loopy softball toss
in a cloud of nightwings, a squadron of beer mugs. A letter
he sent me said I was one of his kind, scribble childish,
slanted as if pinched hard. I wanted to make my world's
rain-huddled boats and bent watermen sound as hurt
as he'd done it. I could always find him if I went where
there was a gasp of hope in a cadence you could join,
bone-jarring like a wooden wagon that still rolled. What
he made you believe was the way they'd hug you in the bar

he never stopped at once. But he knew how it looked, creek
silver as new coins, dirty windows. The redhead? Two kids
in trouble, mortgage, no last name, loved the Yankees
he hated. He might rise from his seat in pain. The hip
bulging his pants? Bomber crash. His grin popped it
back, fooled the orthopedics, too. Come for the reading.
Beer, talk. Once I drove to Michigan for him. He signed
Dick, To one of my kind. We ate a gallon of ice cream,
Mets won in overtime. I just can't do bars anymore, he said.

Christmas Memory

Dave's Finn of Midlothian

The dog followed me belly deep in new snow
I scraped from the sidewalk, a good citizen
trying to follow the rules. He watched the way
he'd pointed birds for me to shoot so many
years, willing to act, faithfully stiff. I saw
him turn back to the porch. Waiting, I thought.
But why? he'd always loved snow play.
How could I know my neighbor, a shadow,
gave him a poisoned gift? The vet asked
why a man would do this. I'd try to answer
sitting where the dog had, shotgun cleaned
on my lap. It was the cold you can dream in,
blinding my face a little. I wanted to see
a shape in the snow appear like a shade-shift.
But I knew enough not to shoot a poor shadow,
not to shoot in my neighborhood, not to be
the kind of asshole who does what he wants
because he can when the gods stop watching.
I knew how my dog had kept his sweet eyes,
his steady nose trued, his silence, his pose,
not fearful, not aggressive, his game to wait,
forgiving himself any false step, flushing
the past until the moment could come just
as it always had. Even days we shot nothing
ended the same, his head on my lap, the drive
I'd make, the heavy weight of him drifting.
But not like that Christmas Day when I lifted
him not out of the car, but into it. Stiffness
not pain, not forgiveness, not the nose in air
where he'd watched what moved, and I had not.

The Horses of Xian

Row upon row of carved stallions time
and earth-weight endow with grace
that pulls still the armies of the Emperor.
Perfect, too, padded vest, lance, brass
wheels no sun can outroll. Warriors
mounted to ride beyond anything alive.

But the fixed step of such battalions—
farriers have told the makers this—
can fade into shriek, a thigh's bone-snap,
one elegant hoof, and the maker drifts
from his poem to pray—no rip
of harness tumbles his finest squadrons

who can go like wind up cliff's breast
or gleam little spruce meadows gold
if fear strikes the gods to hurl them.
But if foreheads seem to tremble
as even great horses do, they dream
they are already charging. Art insists

none think to flee when shapes shift.
The visage of the truest blinks
only once, for these it will be never.
All hooked—fist, saddle, forelock
grip upon blade upon bone—to deliver
what matters—duty's alignments

of flesh, brutes, boys in cocked-up hats.
How could they fail? sculptors boast.
In battle, spit's drip and blood-bubble
perfectly measures a man, the best
horse for field-clamor, the struggle
of hearts buried. See, each pulls for that.

The Planet of Words

Why was I never one to trust a safe snake
flushed from my mother's bed of blossoms,
the sibilant give-and-take of its occupation
surely not the abrupt strike of pain I thought?
Why did spiders bring me fear and malice,
tall-legged black ones, hour-glassed bellies
in the good quiet places where I liked to sit,
a boy wanting to think? Today I picked up
my grandson from school, his classroom full
of coiled creatures so lifeless they might be
only dreams abandoned by those who passed
here, shadows in small hard eyes moving
the way planets do in a sleeper's brain. So I
stopped to look in while my namesake packed,
not thinking a quick tongue meant anything
more than a web, glassy and boxed, meaning
only to kill time. Because so little moved
it seemed like time was dead already. I thought
how once I had sat like him all day waiting.
I must have wanted then what I want now,
a quiet room's forgiveness for what's been
done or not done. I could almost imagine
creatures feeling the same, making ready
bites they'd inflict on people happening by,
especially for the cold coiling-upon-self of
bad self whose fear stunk up thinking places.
Now I gaze over desks in rows, past the blank
faces of children I suspect are watching each
creature as it instructs how to conduct a life.
Do they think about fear? Hurt? What's absent?
I remember when my mother picked me up,
my father gone, the slits of her eyes tight,
wordless dinners, nights like a scaled cage,
life out there coiled where I sat and thought.
The brain spinning like a planet among words.

Grim Permissions

Sometimes the angels on our pond steam
a particularly gold light, skidding electric sun
through the aerating fountain, easy to think
it's a message meant to let us in on doings
of the gods, like a roll call of permissions
we're granted for one day at least. The wren
who's nested on our porch's wicker basket
slips out and brings a full mouth back.
Bass of unusual size plunge up and take all
they can carry. Ducks, geese zigzag smartly,
like a flotilla alert there's something under
the overhead. I like a wooden chair to watch,
coffee or beer depending on the hour, each
event sparking a suspicion about cause. But
vision isn't something sustained very long.
The dragonflies go first, buffeted by the lightest
breeze, then the nattering floaters, and soon
the fountain spray's just a droll doling out.
You can see everything turn, grim, heavy,
looking for home and such explanations as
wait among the tools and plants and hot air.
The wonder is, I suppose, how much we want
to believe we'll hear and see it all tomorrow.
And how we are convinced the world here
stands agreed to perform without regard for
explanation or whatever abuse we may bring.

Dead Calm

When I think of a river, it isn't whitewater,
sleek stones under the surface like hulls
of sunken ships you can take on a mask
and dive to, clear so small fish wait
to see if you have brought good snacks.
Mine has water warm as piss, the salt
taste gags if you swim too long, the lids
of your eyes swell with it, but that's not
the big thing I keep with me. It's the tide

that the moon heaves back and forth twice
every day, a silent wail of water lifting
boats bigger than small towns, shoving
where your house sits unable to believe
the washstand, the beds, the recliner can
be trash a god plays with, walls gasped
surprises as they go blown out. Then
it's like Zeus flicks his feathery finger,
sun boils the bottom bare, stink loves us.

Crabs climb up and down the dock legs,
spot, trout, croaker, even blowfish cruise
where a skiff's shadow dances with lines
you've hung over. Hours, nothing, then
the tide turns, mouths open, they know
the time is short. You know it, too, last
days waiting like shells sharp at flesh,
any slide or fall hurts, fin's bone goes
in deep, a fearful eye blinkless upon you.

Bullfight

The first five died easily, bodies dragged by chains
behind golf carts. The sixth, twisting a horn up,
downed the horse, pinned the rider, then waited as
mounted acolytes jabbed his heart. The matador
in satin slippers, silk pants with rosettes, leveled
one thrust, the bellow brief, then the bloody spit pool.

A middle-aged woman leaped, tossed a rose, hoarse,
calling to the now striding matador. He blinked
and moved on. We followed the crowds, a bar
offered dark faces over slurred plates, frites, steak.
It was like prayer, words we did not use. The horse
they had tarped was admired, and the bull's balls. But

we didn't understand the excitement, only the wine,
and later the sex. Madrid, our bodies probed
in every shadow, every hole, doing all we wanted.
Life is a wonder. We slept, we ate, we made
love, we walked the streets like cows stinking.
One day it all changes. We stopped at the Prado.

A line waited to get in, bodies heavy, sweaty in sun.
Gods in the paintings gazed beyond us, bored.
We saw how their death makes us live as we do.
So much art, so quiet and lonely. I said Fuck.
We ran as if something was chasing us, our room
a glue of dust, of hunger, of the foul smells of bodies.

Monarch

When I wake I reach out to touch my wife
who has left me for the lemon tree trying
to come back from a bad winter. I find her
gazing up so the tree's fullness makes her
face seem old in the sun, lined by shadows
brittle as limbs offering their new leaves.
Today fifty-three years ago we married,
whoever we were lost in the swells we are.
I tap at the window and she turns, points
at Monarch mothers like fiery blossoms.
Polite, patient, they flutter and settle on
still damp leaves coiled like an infant's
fingers, each of them wing-hovering, deft
navigations it takes them lives to learn, then
silvery gray eggs get lodged, and they go.
Wherever they came from, so far away
it can't be seen anymore, has to become
a story to be real. There days vanish,
nights clench each creature until its eyes
pop, and they squint for what hangs on.
Many spray them, my wife says, I can't.
Tiny. Ashen. But the distance they move is
a river's breath relentless with cavitation,
until their bodies, too, swell and expel like
moon glitter on old, bending limbs. She's
merciless as the clock, snipping and pruning,
thorns razoring her ungloved knuckles. Sun,
the brutal suitor, blinds me from her gaze,
so I tap again, plead my love. When she sees
who's come, black-spotted leaves shaking
at her fingertips, she lifts it between us.
Jesus, her mouth says, what a beautiful day.

Visiting the Scottish Poet

for Douglas Dunn

At St. Andrews the double-decker ducked
down a country road, blue like my wife's eyes,
bushes I couldn't name, oozing Spring, whoosh
to a handful of roofs, glaze of rain, a wall
where the poet appeared. He lived alone,
wife, kids elsewhere. Tea, cakes, dishes mismatched.
His garden table, words warm as for old chums,
Burns in situ, but soon talk turned, well, slow,
life not real in words we used. I recalled
his wife, vivid painter. I'd recited his poems
to Dee. "He's lonely," she said as afternoon
steeped his garden's plants. Some burdened others
as if wilder, bolder. We drank scotch, walked
to his brook, a stone wall. Dee, half-interested,
asked what was on the far side. He blinked
as Jesus might, if asked. "Sir Sean Connery—,"
he said. My wife's red lips made a sharp "Oh,"
as if she'd entered a dream. Our last day
wasted with poets, worrying words, gossip,
unreal, she'd said, so boring! Wasn't there more?
But now I saw her touch the long-stem rose,
cup blossoms in palms, and gaze across the brook.
Too late for a walk-over, I said, and took
her hand and took us to the bus back. The poet
kissed her goodbye, a prince. "Perfect," she said,
as we droned home, past faces sitting alone.
She might have been, but wasn't, dreaming I was
a man unseen, she was the woman leaving
a garden no love could exhaust. "Perfect."
In mocking brogue I answered her. "Like a poem."
"Dearest," she said, kissing me as a dream does.

Hopeless Dog

My bird dog points, summer heat at the door,
ready to knock aside anyone in his way, sure
to snatch in his teeth the unwariest lizard
that flashes, as they do here, on garden floors.
I know how he feels, that muscle that's desire
balling up like an aging hamstring, pupils
so tensed their black watch is like a wizard's.
But these are not birds, these green mouthfuls,
just beautiful bellyaches he'll vomit like fire.
If I tie him, he chews free, the garden chairs
get toppled, he'll stand hours, wand of his tail
rigidly trembling at shadows, his dick revealed.
How helpless we are, oh death's runners,
who tease us like magic, like dreams we endure.

Lizards Running

I don't understand the violence of men
who bring screams to a child by tossing it
against a concrete garage wall, the butts
of drinkers, the young girl raped. I don't
understand how two men jump from Ford
pickups same age different color punches
start flying in the intersection we want
only to pass through, our dinner waiting.
I don't know how I didn't understand
if I put my hand in the mailbox blindly
the wasps would feel I might have reason
to harm them, so I got more than my mail.
In Syria, Somalia, the Ukraine, deadeye
middle-school kids pick up the pieces
of their cousins so somebody will know
who is not coming home. They don't ask
what the bomber looked like, they don't
watch the window at night as the moon
pushes their faces under cloth scarves.
Maybe I understand they run for cover
the way green lizards do if a bird comes by.
In my town after dinner lazy summer night
slides through the solemn streets where we
used to chase the mosquito truck, gagged
by sweet fog we didn't know was deadly.
Soon the faint popping of drive-by shots.
They don't stay long. Afterward voices
angry, muffled shouts, somebody slams
a door hard. That's all. Time to go stand
on the moon's porch and listen. The buzz
of insects is like a big breath let out slowly.
It's not painful, just something I understand.

One or the Other

I see the father carry the bloody body of a child
maybe ten years old, age of my four grandsons,
he's in the street looking for the way to go, it's
shaking the TV camera, whatever makes powdery
the air this man wears on his raked face, and he
can't choose which way. The boy doesn't mind,
his head hangs, eyes open, he might be just awake,
on the way to his grandmother's and new sweets,
or maybe he's entered a dream and won't leave it,
though the man shakes him now and again, looks
down over the face, as if he can't remember a thing.
I want to grab him by the ears and drag him where
the road slips under thick, green limbs, the rose
of the evening sky as welcoming as his wife's lips.
I want to tell him whatever he hears it is the gods,
those motherfuckers who like to steal a good skin
and tear it slowly inch by inch, making their bets
you can't cause them to stop, not with fist, not
with prayer, not with scream, not even with tears
they love to drink up more than rotgut whiskey.
I want to tell him they are no joke, waiting on
tees of golf courses, building big houses in fields,
whisking past in cars more beautiful than stallions
born to know where to go for no reason, who go
and leave us behind in dreams with no words.

New Neighbor

A man down the street comes to befriend me,
knocks on my door, hangs out
talking on my porch, the government
sucks, retirement sucks, maybe
I might have seen him fishing our lake.
I see the pond glary and sullen behind him.

Doves coo in shadows. It hasn't been good
today, words clotted like the bottom
of my garbage can, water oaks
dropping leaves I can't keep up with,
I dream of a young woman
saying I'm in love with you, who are you

sleeping with besides me? I don't complain
when he keeps talking, I see the box
he cradles to me, his wife's cake. It's time
I'm losing. I think of Bernard Malamud
at a writers' conference crying free
chocolate cakes they come with worms,

and his wife Ann at his reading, Bern, enough
already, the crowd laughing. Tiny man,
huge glasses, his big bellyache
later at the party turned out serious.
Also Richard Ellman saw moon soldiers
crawl toward us, meds not taken. You

a writer? the man says. So here's cake.
I see he also carries a fly rod, Orvis, a fake
cast shivers toward my wife's car.
I practice casting, he says. You? I see
dusk is coming, but I think he could be
Jesus, I don't want to get on the wrong foot.

I say, I might have a beer if you want one.
I say we might have pretzels.
I can see Bern retching, Richard's crazy
words in the moonshine. Next time
he says, backing away. You like golf?
I nod. I can't think of anything to say.

A Sunday Story

Today Dee calls to tell me she loves me
and am I all right? This happens while I am
sweating enormously on the local golf course,
an outing with my grown son to watch me
in case of diabetic seizures I sometimes have.
It's Sunday morning, you might think it's
ordinary, a man not praying who is playing
on God's time gets a call from a woman
thousands of miles away, visiting a grandson.
Are you alright? Jesus, she sighs. The TV
news here says people are shooting up cops
there—where are you? In Baton Rouge people
are dead on the road I go down every day. Where
are you, my dear one? I am on the seventh
hole, my putt's lined up, you never call me so
I answer, maybe it's important, but can it wait?
Sweetheart, she says, I love you, I'm coming
back soon, are you alone, shouldn't you go home,
don't answer the door, drink a cold beer, maybe
ask some of the neighbors to visit? I see my son
duff his putt, hurry to the next tee, wanting now
to see his own son, he's waving a white towel
as if to distract my dismay. What can I do?
I start walking faster but go on listening because
the time it will take for waiting for my love
to return begins to seem impossibly longer than
the time any of us has left, it's brutally hot, too.
I've started thinking about voices, bodies, shots,
children wailing, and that absolute silence
that settles on a golf course once you're done.
Night soothes the trees, sirens fade into distance.
Under such circumstances it's hard to see faces

driving home, a face nobody ever calls again,
a face trying to remember what you looked like
making a good putt, whooping, hugging a son.
And always the feel of the cool smooth grass.

Looking Up

Some things in life have no good explanation.
A seam of mold on our bedroom's cathedral
ceiling—was it a way-back fault, bad roof,
promise I hadn't cared for as I should ? Oh
I did nothing but worry until at last I saw this
smear might end us, just big enough waking
lovers might see it, faint as guilt, first thing
each morning. Dreams said, What can you do?
No house broom, no poking stick reached
the irritant I had to scrub. A pole and sponge
appeared too short, too weak. Like excuses.
Yet as one thing leads to another, an extension
ladder came in from the garage. I leaned this
on the six-footer, believing I was solid. My wife
by now was off in the garden, calm as the sun,
her love planting and watering in perfect trust.
I understood what was at stake and I wasn't
the man I used to be, a sly climber, but I knew
the stain had to go. I believed in a man's will.
With knots of twine for hanging our tomatoes
I fixed me in place. How could I fail? I knew
what I knew might doom our last days. Fix it,
my brain said, desperate, unable to see how
I could not fail to fall, but no hope otherwise.
So up I went, worming my way, offering all
to this marriage. One touch wasn't enough,
I stretched more, again more, pushed, swabbing
what wouldn't quit, until it seemed almost gone.
Then boom! twine snapped, ladder flung, I flew
ten feet, bounced on bed's gullied heart, old
man hurting, scared, alive. What had I done?
That's when my love's anxious voice came,
it asked for explanations, and you have to say.
I gave all the details, it took time, in the light
of that day turning to night and then more days

where she gazed past me up to the dark place.
We'll get it fixed, she said, her hand pointed
to pull me upright, her smell of sweat and dirt
mysterious as love that redeems as it forgives.

Prophecy

So many years I did not wander the world,
I stayed in my room with walls of words.
I read the great poets, the so-so-poets,
dead poets whose books I gave to libraries
to raise money for the poor. The work of
poetry left my skin mottled like vellum,
my once-handsome legs bowed by desks,
back warped like the dried-up bonsai bush
a woman gave me, saying it's pure poetry.
The older I got the less poet I seemed to be.
Routine examinations showed the wild
in me had withdrawn like a low tide.
My heart beat so slowly a nurse called
the doctor to see if I was in trouble. I was
dreaming the life of words, my head hurt
with questions I could not answer—the nature
of gods, what makes character, is a poem
lying with truth? I dreamed of waking
in the arena of people whose hands filled
with pencils, planes, hammers, spirit levels.
Are you rich enough to pay? the nurse said.
Insurance, I said, a vision of human plenty.
She spoke then in edged, indecipherable words
not unlike those of a lover who asks if you,
and when, and how often. I understand,
I said, but truly I did not, for what happens
confuses, mystifies all of us. I kept thinking
how Jesus said have no concern for money.
Then the doctor held my hand, it was weird.
I could hear him counting quiet as a priest.
You ought to be dead, he told me. Nurse
says you're a poet, so save you. My wife
writes poems. Now he had his cold gizmo
on my chest. Breathe deep, he said, again,
his lunch, spicy, mortgaged, embracing me.

Silent Movie

This is the last house I will ever live in,
I thought, my hand on the brass knob,
but hadn't I thought that each time before?
And always it was the same house only
different paint, doors moved around some,
the front porch with wasps? The neighbor?

It wasn't hard to remember coming home,
locked out, knock bringing the new owner.
It's you, he said, your mother said expect
a bewildered young man who's lost
his father. He blinked at me like a crow.
He said your mother married, she's gone.

I couldn't understand what we were saying.
So we said it all again. Same old blue
sky, same pine trees, the grass I mowed,
silent as ever, Mr. Cross across the street
in his rocker watching, the leg he lost
still rotting, nose like a pecked corncob.

He waved when I climbed in a car and left.
Who knew I was the poor boy in his head,
one who'd keep coming back, words
clumping on tongue, eyes darting, black
as nights roosting on hard, distant limbs?
What do you say to a dead neighbor's wave?

You walk the upchucked concrete path, go
direct to the face blank as an executioner's,
push palm out, hear summer bugs scream.
It's all in your head, it's nothing real.
Don't trip, don't mumble, think movie.
Whatever happens, they're all dead now.

Suckers

Never give a sucker an even break.
—W. C. FIELDS

We have a neighborhood truly connected
by website and email, a communion of
pleas comes every day to fully understand
why a cottonmouth wants so to transcend
any fence yard-keepers erect, or how holly
berries transform into glass shivers when
a dog eats them. There's a classified part
listing what goes to the curb this morning:
headless dolls, old bikes, bookcases still
painted with that hippy gladness, and you
can see the startled gaze of the black man
who looks into a door-bell eye, the woman
inside feeling her nerve ends go like piss
a dog has just driven from a wandering cat.
So many cats and dogs appear in the weepy
messages, some leaving home, some lost
but found and now held for pick-up, some
just dropped into the world, that the gods
must have imagined new torture for suburbs.
Technology has given them utter promise
for the great and fiery sparks they always had,
so the cute names, the furry plate-eyes leap
from house to house like a plague of ticks.
But the gods, always smart, don't overdo it.
They know what it's like to be turned off,
boxed in, merely shadows padding, worlds
of light closed down at the slightest sound.
That's why they give every dog a name,
no matter the despair in its eyes, you reach
the hand a pussy would comfort, no matter
you know it's not a good idea. All of them
want to be home for the night, go belly up

in your mind as soon as the email flashes.
Beware! The gods know what suckers are.
Who invented "Have a good day"? The gods.
And who invented dreams and webites?
And space, and time, and pity. Oh, suckers.

III.

Seizure

for Stephen Dunn

Walking the dog before dawn, alone in the blue rain
of Louisiana, I come face to face with a family
loss, chunks of floors, molding, plastic dollhouse—
the house dark as despair. Floods come easy here.
But from the pile a bent metal arm sticks up,
as if saying *Fuck it, enough!* So I kneel and see
what was someone's walker is, now, not even
a last slow-motion scrape in a sinking house. I say

move on, don't be helpless, blood sugar falling.
I feel my legs leave me so bite candy I carry,
chew the wrapper,wait. I think someone has to be
left, who ripped and carried out what was sweet
like life once. Sugar's everything, the way love is,
a whistling lingo that half explains why I've looked
up, knocked down in the street, shuddering, a girl
kneeling, pushing her strawberry cone to my lips.

What's shaking, man, a man said, dog sniffing, but
both gone before I could say, me, man, words
in my mouth sloshing like water, tongue like glass
where windows burst, floor buckles. Accept it:
bad things happen to all of us, my friend mused.
But now I need someone to step from that house.
His walker sticks up like a hand, seize it, you can
then help me stand, friend. Look, it might work!

It's all about living with trouble, my friend said,
who let himself go. I understand it's hard to wait
like damage on the street. Maybe no one will stop,
bend down, touch. Maybe no ice cream or juice.

But I've seen a stranger lift me, I've heard love
run in the night to say You're still alive, my dear.
That walker? Friend, think of it as an arm offered,
another and another, chaining. Steps. More steps.

Man Swimming in Home-Dug Pool

His card came, who is dead now, "Come swim."
At woods sky-freckled, log ladder
to bottom, I heard him saying "Lycidas."
The pond, a hole long dammed, made
by shovels rusted under leaf-fall, is night-black.
At first you don't see the old man. Then spidering

over a cradled slickness of newts, minnows,
unknown striders, he sees you, hand
climbs edge, then translucent body,
blue veins like a ghost scripture, hauls up.
The once-white robe curls, lifts,
peels about him like a snakeskin. I don't know

what to call him. He waves me up. "Yes Sir."
All I know to do is follow. How strange,
I recall, boy's black Speedo, gut ball, woman's
bathing cap. Up hill, at the edge we climb
into the noon. There he stops, turns,
leans on my car, parked in weeds, looks back.

His gaze leads mine, the unfinished hole, scary,
so ordinary it looks, but not. Steps go
from living house, past coop-house for writing,
nothing to see except the slip-ledge
where he launched. Now I am his age
then, and his voice hurled up from that water.

Seasons he swam, in snow, stars, bird whistle, or
dead quiet. His kids moved on, with kids.
Did they not swim? Maybe that's why
he rummaged a suit for me,
baggy, old-style, but decent enough.
Voice like gravel pushed, he said, Jump in, son!

Old arms, feathered like a hawk's, later lifted
two chairs, glasses he filled, then stories,
grandfathers, soldiers, bankers, but
nameless because, as he said, they float out
of an old man's mind. But what
a thing man is, he had said. In his own poem.

We talk on the porch, late, but not yet dinner,
I see him reach my new book, he breaks it
open, red scribblings like a map.
What, I think, could I have to say to him?
Points finger, says fix this. Yes sir, but
what is *it?* I hear my breath slow, trying to track *it*.

When she calls, he says you hate to quit. But he
rises, goes. I walk into trees, piss my
name, as once my father showed me, and dress
in my car for dinner. With tie. Two owls
measure darkness and discuss it. What
had he wanted from me? At dinner, beyond guests

he glared, kept wordless, face pinched, seeking.
His wife with tales recalled him, old fool
climbing a camel, his paper stash
for toilet. Here she touched his arm, but he was
mid-air, at pond, bodies, stars, where
all swirled, as if an entrance opened. Diving.

Door closed, night-drive, high stars, and in bed
I talked to my wife—why was I there, what
strangeness that face floating from
words, like dream. Arms up like a man
surrendering, him vanishing, who had said, Go
to the bottom not touched, touch *it*. Look up. Push *it*.

The Thief of Small Toys

A mechanical frog that hopped, wound up, its spring twisted
as if a god, going to work, killed it with a shoe.
Gods do that. On my desk the 1963 Corvette,
our first car, sat patient all the years, one
door open, black, sleek as dreams we had when
we married, running as far away as we could. Remember?

A yellow woodpecker, tin, whose only skill was a rhyme
pecked at whatever world it strode. Two or three tiny
soldiers, Stars Wars AWOL, our son's, tipped over.
A German trapeze man, exhausted, moped.
Stuffed birds our dog gutted, the Chesapeake Bay
log canoe scaled so fitly it seemed seaworthy forever.

Toys were the best, cheap companions to keep on shelves
full of poems. They'd spin, chime, roll or just watch.
Owl staring, one-eyed crow—who'd want what
kids gave us? High so they couldn't be lost—gone.
I run my hands where I can't quite see.
The only thing left is poets I once read, spine by spine

So I take one down, as if past brooding dust may be
some clue, some Aha! the old poems held,
then take down another, and another—but lines
blur like a burglar's lies. Where are hops, croaks,
cranks of wheels bearing joy we imagined?
What good is a poem that can't tell us what happens?

Still I like to sit where little things once held you and me.
Summer days, cities blinked—we were *there?* Then
the sob of our child, her doll lost. Then the toys
on morning's floor and we lifted them up,
weightless and worn to wait there with words
I liked to read, written by people still playful and wise.

Breakable Jesus

Twilight in moss-draped spruce brings the glazed
look of things seen through tears. Lulu's book
splays in her lap, gold hair like a mist, she plays
at my feet, talking to no one as a vision does.
She's gathered her stuffed animals, arranged them
as if in pews, a half-circle of breathless worship.
From some back drawer or box we once stashed,
a figurine has come among them, cold ceramic
face, fragile, but sure eyes, the man of calendars
in the stores of my childhood. Holding a hand,
my grandmother's maybe, I see myself in a gaze
older than we will ever be. I feel the promise
not only of safety or love but a care I was more
wholly in than anything alive. Let go in the dime
store, old woman a shadow near me, I wandered
to touch toys, dream the roles each one offered,
learning costs, choices, a blunt sword, cheap
plastic car, dinosaur with teeth big as our trees.
Late, late I would lie waiting to sleep as voices
talked on, certain my dreams would end exactly
as they told me, day's light, the good breakfast,
wooden floor under my naked feet. I'd wash,
then I might gaze at the little Jesus, lifting it,
until the kind voice said that's breakable, son,
and we won't get another. The face sun-cracked,
mole-flecked, haloed with fine hair, seemed to me
the same as one hung on the barber shop's wall,
school, or Casteen's Pure station where the voice
said pee, I'll get gas. Time came, I didn't see it
anymore, or didn't recognize it, so imagined it
left us. Now here it is again, the face I see made
in China, whose long hair Lulu's sadly chipped.
I rock with coffee as she commands the room
to hear what Jesus says to animals who maybe
are not breakable yet but might get to be. So

do you know what breakable means, I ask her.
She says only "I know," trying to imagine
what danger is already in the room with us.
As the power in dream does, holding its tongue.

Muse Story

My friend David Huddle imagines a poem's
muse as one of the birds auditioning
in his garden, a small but ferocious voice
nobody sitting among the ferns can turn
away from. It's worse if you stand at glass
keeping the snow and brilliant holly berries
outside, in a teasing swirl of ice-wind, say.
I like his thinking. I've felt bird spirits
fly inside my head, songs trying to get out,
some controller watching the time, a faceless
spark-dodging denizen of a really dark place
not letting happen what shouldn't yet. She,
that's how I think of this monster, can swell
a huge room with a sound an angel would
screw you to have. She can whisper the way
a snowflake does falling still at last, you
only have to feel her hands hover to know
whatever she touches will turn out better
than the best orgasm you'll ever dream.
I think the sidelong look she has is a hawk's,
the glance a hummingbird's beak, but for
full-on character display that's her rising,
owl-skim just above your skull, talons
held up barely enough as she soars from a tree.
She could touch you anytime and your brain
blister out like a rose, your tongue turn hard
as holly blackened by winter. I don't think
a man chooses in this story. Maybe a cloud
of them arrives Thursday night. They have to
do something to you then, and then flee, all
except the one who chooses you, listening.
There's no accounting for taste, someone's
bent over laughing where yours comes from.
Jesus Christ, someone's saying. Really, him?

Now That I Am Dead

Now that I am dead under the azaleas
colorful as a woman's wedding gown,
below dirt just heaped, what good is love?
I made such noise about feeling I was
lonely, misery-ridden, badly done-to,
I made myself sick and turned to words
twisted into little songs I liked to hum.
Women in glasses often asked for more,
crossing their legs, watching the windows.
Whatever they said, they said love is
why a man wants a new car, why songs
and home towns are always waiting for him
to walk in disguised as wisdom and sex.
The story is people can't get enough jokes
to chain them together, laughing, crying
until the man goes into a bar, the woman
snorts, sixty minutes you're dreaming,
and the barman snickers oh stop it now
as the dark ending slips through a side door,
sleek bitch quickly gone with someone else,
and day ticks, clicks on like the streetlight.
So there I was, lifting the foamed glass,
trying to remember who I had ever loved,
and who might have loved me when
the lovers walked in, took a quiet booth,
spoke a few words, then one took it out
and bang! missed the other, but got me.
It's that randomness I miss most of all,
the way love filled in the cracks of a day,
or showed up in a bar all normal looking
but already crazy, already the squeeze
not you, not them, not anyone alive keeps.

Fatigue

Today I power-washed the porch, sun boiled
so once I had to lay flat-out. I swear
in that blinding fuse of light the angels
whipped around me like cloggers
in a county bar. That sort of thing is
enough to set your mind reaching. Mine
found a black-clad blonde with stick, a lank

one with the walk of a girl, au naturel, sweet
bounce on the foot's ball, the sway of air
in a hot room. I could feel her breath
pass words in and out of my ear, maybe
proposing we get locked. Fifty years
(why that number?) or so looked
to me like utter fatigue, maybe her age.

I held out. But in due course it was woods,
blossoms I can't name but sweet odor,
damp earth on my pants' knees, the good
time loved by all. I think now of old
Flaubert who claimed a night of three
coups, diary gibberish with pride, while
I imagined four, even leaves applauding.

Strange memory is that lies and never wants
to claim quiet nights with a snoring muse.
More, more, I proclaim, lying on
my back, wanting each angel going by,
her radiant look a sure contract.
I'll be as hard as the earth that holds me.
Surely she believes that who once came for me.

A Horse Named Jesus

How blessed horses smell . . .
—JIM HARRISON

for Lael and Mary

Daughters, I sit dreaming, what I know of horses
a scum-faced pond tells me today, how we
often remember love that hurt us. Both of you
rode Jesus summers past, you wore the smell
of him when you came or went, that fecund robe
of fields you passed, afraid, small, chosen
ones he carried, a sorry god with gruffs of breath.

By tether tamed, he swirled girls in circles, each
learning lean and speed and grace to be
upright in all respects, faces blank as mares who
watched in old barn stalls. Legs locking,
arms fluttery as butterflies, you rode the way
a dream does, holding on. Beneath you,
he conjured a passage docile as a bishop's rites.

Except that one day we saw him hunch, buck loose
you from his stirrups, for no reason, dust
swallowing you, blood, knees ripped, a mean fall.
Had he meant such harm? Above you then
he stood unblinking, accepting, flies his tail swept
like our fears. You rose, took reins, and kicked
as if now he was yours. Now that rank horse let go

a burst of piss, heaping gold shits, each hoof a storm
of bad dreams of Jesus who came to ride you.
Year after year they walked, horse, daughters, stink
we called the ever-after. He was our living myth.
But time came, he kicked, squealed, he blew up,
in pain, a biter, the ineluctable sliding forth.
Who loved my daughters the way God loved him.

Rain Play

Today a man I play golf with stopped me
to ask how it was going, and I thought
how I'd endured his unbearable habit
of hanging a portable radio on his bag,
hole after hole of country music, most
of us too weak to say we want some quiet,

enough gabble about so many abandoned,
those cheating drunks and dreamers,
hearts all but cut out of chests, words
spinning and wobbling to a bad end
like balls we hit one after another. But
won't suffering teach us to dream away

failure, hurt, pain they sing so sweetly?
So I said I was going ok, never better,
as if it was true, making us nod together.
I didn't ask about his son's cancer or
his dead wife, or when we'd play again.
Like Hemingway, I walked off in the rain.

You remember the novel's end? True, but
unbelievable, like guitars and big hats.
Like finding yourself in a pastel golf shirt
bizarrely striped, driving home, cleats on.
"I'll see you." Thinking about rain, mud,
the hope you'll play tomorrow. "Take care."

For the Birds

My walls pile books to the ceiling, mostly poets,
some the fat accumulation of memoirs, more
the thin, brittle clutch of words that now lean
upon the shoulders of another. There's little
rhyme or reason, no story to tell in most cases,
they don't know how they got here, I can't say,
all of them given to me by time and friends.
I've tried to be generous in return, thousands
passed on to students, book-buyers, the poor
who linger in thrift stores with the used shoes.
I've come on my own books there, signed
to poets I once knew. I could redeem them,
give them again, but maybe they'd come back,
I'd have to see what I said, and to whom, how
could I bear what no one wanted enough to keep?
There's a finch nested on our porch, five eggs
the size of my fingernail, nest perfectly mounded
so they remain a secret until startled, voices
she leaves, returns to regular as a blood-beat.
I'd like to ask her what the point is, to hear
assumptions, speculations, the itch of theory
that lays twig by twig into what she will flee.
Recent days I've seen her cling to the wooden
ledge of my window, wings humming, head
canted as if to read the titles fading in the sun.
Maybe the gods sent her to check on things
we don't understand well enough. The bold
authority of her voice, outsize and commanding,
seems to rise inside my body, unchosen, lovely.
But I could be mistaken, she might be a poet
singing lies so impeccable they turn out the truth.

Depth of Pond

Today a summer storm scrambled the face
of our pond, lightning, wind hurling the small
spears of cypress like aborted ideas. Then
a cool clearing time, the thrushes strutting
and a couple of cardinals hopping for insects,
the water murky as an old man's coffee. I
like to go to the edge where debris settles.
Some people want the depths made visible,
perhaps missing what cannot be used anymore,
perhaps wanting to explain to the blank-faced
all that the rest of us leave to the gods. But
if you stand at the edge so the small movers
and delicate shapes agree to reveal a little,
it doesn't seem so awful and it welcomes you
with everything in its place, clear, still strong,
just as the makers of storms must have wanted.
Pond, here I am, I like to say. Take me now.
I do it the way I was taught to invite Jesus,
remembering how I closed my eyes not to
see what was happening. Later, trying to sleep,
I felt something big had watched me, but I
was not ready to be ferried away. Oh depth,
oh pond, I said, open to me the most secret
things cast with you. Broke-neck wood duck,
carbuncled carp, half of a dog, neighbor's
pirogue that once, at its end of chain, rubbed
a hole and sank in it. It's all here, the gods
slide it under the muck my feet hide in, they
ask you to come look but they don't reveal.
Jesus, oh Jesus, you say, as if they all have
the one name, and that storm? It's laughter.

The Secret of Herd Travel

Led by the big-antlered grandfather, fur stained
by age and new mud, the others crossed
the field next to our yard. They stood
in the silver dew more like a dream than grass.
We were eating breakfast, in hunger's gaze-lock.

My grandson had seen them before, his moon-eyes
settling on each, then tracking as if puzzled.
He could count his fingers and toes,
so maybe he understood the missing one,
its small shape dark red on our road where living

only looked changeless. The boy asked me where
dead ones went, who'd leaped over to eat
with us all summer. He wanted to go
call them from the woods where some must be
hiding from trucks, saws, voices building houses.

Mostly we kept quiet, spooning in our cereal as deer
lifted and lowered their heads, watching us
as if they knew an answer we did not,
nosing the grass delicious and endless.
After a while I asked him if he had more questions.

Why? He said. I could see he was thinking it over.
What would we do after the herd went away?
Hammers tapped from shade, enough
to frighten a waking boy. I rubbed his head.
We could go somewhere, Pop, he said. For lunch.

Already the hooves flowing back over our road
seemed bigger leaving, the heads fewer.
The boy ate toast clotted with jelly.
We washed in the sink, chins lifted, dripping.
If we dream, or do not, hunger comes. So we eat.

Reading Obituaries

Dee asks me to write my obituary, reasoning
she will have to do it if death gets me first.
What is the point? I ask, resisting questions
neither my life nor death will answer. Why
did he do that, was she wronged? And who
will open his newspaper to say, Guess what?
That poet fellow in Louisiana? He left us.
I sit at the pond Fall's shined like a mirror
full of what is happening with no one's notice.
Mallards zigzag, dying leaves drift, the faces
of the newly gone open my morning paper.
I read each memory of good days, a mystery
of crows echoes from oaks like old squadrons
calling up their decorations, schools attended,
first marriages, seconds, last. Can they teach me
what's right to say in death's story? All smile.
No love scars, no tortured souls, no choice
that stabs year after year. Yet I see they loved
fishing, travel, the dog named Wife, the wife
named Dog, so I try to focus the wit of it all.
I grin at the news so many fought the good
fight, "livered hard, hopped (sic) to see Jesus."
Across the way a dog stops, pisses another's
piss spot, sniffs air, journeys on, and I think
of faces clenched on mantels, ashes blown,
briefly stuck on pond top, on sunken pirogue
so you wonder what happened. Or stare as I do
where someone slams a car door twice. Hard
life, Jesus, some had, what words savor it well?
I keep starting and restarting, bullied by costs,
connections, meanings of the done and undone.
Should I quote? Scripture? Writers? Dreams
I lived? I walk to the pond edge where muck
settles, life-shapes rise. Our bigmouth bass
looms, his gills are black fans. Like angels

minnows flash in his mouth. None skid aside.
Sometimes, the quiet awful, I begin to hear
laughter in houses, serious stories revising
redemption, love's faces fixed. When Dee
calls me in, I'll sip whiskey, we'll eat, dream,
truth-talking all night, death too bored to listen.

Memorial

Today on the 17th fairway I stepped over
the gutted, dried-out corpse,
not quite the length of my arm once,
now more papery shell than any
fish, and yet moccasin still.
The triangular head had been halved,
a six-iron maybe, swung without thought.
Twisting tongue gone into this grass,
making for the pond maybe,
that was gone too, the way words go
when we open our mouths
and try to remember what we have done.
So little of it all really matters.
Sunlight poured down its free admiration,
a scale here and there gleamed
as if a nerve had been touched again,
so we stood off even as we bent our backs
to understand more. You know, don't
you, our brains were saying, they will bite
you even when they are dead? But
look how there was an eye, a beauty.
Braided and subtle was what covered
this rippling, this surge to go over
to the side it couldn't see,
turning as the planet does, slow, sure.
Instant by instant it must have
blinked, tasted, filled itself with knowing
it would have to kill some things
to get where the future would be better.
Sometimes it would lie in the grass,
rain falling with its voice of approval,
but always the thump and rumble.
Until the dark, and then endless sun
its body would hold like a scaled straw.

Quail

Darkling, I listen . . .

—JOHN KEATS

1.

With Mary Catherine, maybe ten, I walked.
Then a diabetic seizure came, down I went
face-first in woods. I only meant to show
where a covey lived, what a flush was like,
to say how a pup might follow flyers too far,
who at dusk called like family to be found.
She knew enough to bolt for help, and did.
Soon stars were like nails shooting down.
She beat on suburban doors and said I'd die.

2.

Was she wrong? Maybe. I meant to show her
the little I knew. I walked that creek, her age,
and wanted her to feel the life I felt pulling
us like rhymes. I knew the deep ditch bank
once held trees sky-high with blind ways.
Small life needs such cover to survive. But
tracks of diggers, backhoes, graders now
sent quail more out of sight than ever. Look,
I said, we have to go deep to find them, so had.

3.

The dead taught me to let them rise, gun up,
dog held by words soft-said. She followed.
Pull slow, they said. Dog does the rest. Yes,
seductions of the past killed pretty good.
Add tractors dragging out the guts of swamps,
saws whining through trees, daily hammers

that roof it all in, little wonder the wildest
covey stands less with us than mastodons.
We walked beyond the barbecues and mowers.

4.

Surely death's the cost of happiness. At home
as kids we ran behind bug-truck clouds, summer
gagging our cries out, whistles for the family
be-bop of bobble-notes. We'd call quail until
they stopped answering. Then they'd call us
like wild dreams, voices not heard for years.
But that day I heard it, old hunger, and went.
What but death kept that one bird live? Mary,
watch, learn, I said. She'd heard, and followed.

5.

Years keep in us a local mind to remember
where we lived, a vision of family, why we sing.
Sometimes I stand in my yard, and listen, alive
because those scattered bird-notes saved me,
calling to other hearts come home. *Come now.*
So Mary came, Jesus, with someone's apple juice.
How does a man say what life's gift feels like?
It's in joyful sounds the tongue finds, desperate,
as when a quail cries, here I am love, *Come now.*

A Hurricane Story

Our almost-instinct almost true:
What will survive of us is love.
    —PHILIP LARKIN

When summer afternoons get black, I look out
where water is coming. Soon I remember home.
A waterman I knew took to his rocker when storm
tore reed-tops, and dockyards, and laundry hung,
a nightmare even gods can't explain. He retired
thinking of all the days he'd been out in water's
troughs smacking, lodged gear, lifted feet, rocked,
tried to pray, no answer, so wished for his old boat
lunging, whiskey in it he would have drunk. Except
he was loved, so he promised the woman. Power
out the little radio wouldn't sing even the hillbilly,
it was just the black tide to watch, coming, taking.
Like the only road they had, the floor went under,
they lost the mailbox, then his pants, her dress gone.
They saw little crabs, panicked, swim under the bed.
He pissed in the sink, had to go. It looked like soup.
The woman hummed against awful quiet. He said
hurricane changes how things sound. Kept rocking.
I saw how he'd lean, pause to listen as a waterman
does floating all his life. What he hears is dismay.
He wouldn't say that word, so small. But knows
when it's come in the house, planks warp, popping
off like bottoms of boats wedged in marsh. Boots
fill on his feet, it smells like swamp gas, the rocking
is done, there's pee and shit all over, faces waiting,
calls for children, parents, her dog—all floating close.
He isn't afraid, he's been drunk, alone, fallen in it,
washed up on a marsh cove, mud-stiff, as if dead.
But heard gospel voice, or gull. Something. And if
whatever comes next isn't worse, he said, I'll live.
But black glass she stared at, wind that stayed in

her head, some things she's said, they were worse,
forgetting my name, the bed where she used to go.
I can see her face in his, like love he remembers.
It was when whoever of hers hadn't come home,
storm, we first done it, she made slick fillet, said
don't pee in my soup pot, just keep rocking, you.
Worse than a hurricane, he said, when you have to go.

IV.

Tomatoes

When I eat a tomato I look at it the way anyone else would.
But when I paint a tomato, then I see it differently.
—HENRI MATISSE

for Dee

1.

When I was a boy near the salt marshes, I liked to see
a red-winged blackbird dive like a Navy jet from Norfolk.

Wing-flash and swoop-out, the landing stuck, held
swaying on marsh grass so slim
it glittered, an angel's tether to the world.

Head tilted as if hearing the voice of a god it couldn't locate,
black as the swamp muck swaddling the roots of all I loved,
clenching plants, workboat working alone.

Three or four of them, an orchestra.
Each bright patch a sign
on the shoulder red as a ripe tomato.

Sweet call over water a small lightning.

2.

The old man in the field beside our rented house had two lives.
When he drank, he wrestled the night with awful sounds.
Days, he rode the Ford tractor up and down
crying for his love until sleep came after him.

He climbed down on knees that creaked, he knelt
by the wood barrel he had once packed crabs in.
Here rain water steeped, no fin now,

and he scooped with a silvery bucket what waited for him,
the wet darkness his handkerchief went to, lifted,
and held at forehead as a girl in love might do.

Then he squeezed out what afternoons on the tractor left
upon him, cloth taking it away,
barrel restoring his blood.
Mornings his staked rows bulbed green and heavy.

3.

At kitchen window, under sill, a yellow spider swayed weaving
home, her silks feathered over the barrel's crabsmelling
slats, crushed oyster shell path, black ground

he plowed, watered, as the woman said, to make tomatoes,
leaves coiled like baby fingers. He liked
to unroll and sing them open. Tiny

first blossoms yawed away when his gourd, a big one,
poured a silvery stream that bubbled and broke,
the grass at window dewed up with beads

his wife had worn long ago. I glowed with love then, he'd say.
His seaman's shoulders, his bald dome,
even his frog-heavy face, sun-fired, shook a little.

He'd hunch past our *Ligustrum* hedge, hat cocked, straw basket
battered, but great red globes the load he carried.

4.

Well, what is a man supposed to do? He asked. Well, let us see,
he said, who touched and sliced, slurped and spread
before us baroque as a painter's dreams
amazing tomatoes.

They hang and sweat, timeless, they swell
with redness like my wife's lips that I love,
their names bring the marsh breeze.

Beefsteak, Big Boy, pink Brandywine, purple Cherokee,
Early Girl, Little Cherries,
but his best, Virginia's Hanover—

soft in the hand like a breast.

Stew-makers, pasta-pleasers, with salt, sometimes fried—

I liked them in a sea of vinegar and cucumbers.
I liked them with clouding onions in rings.
I liked to pick them at sunset, blackbirds on the low limbs.
I liked to see them float in the darkness, him walking on.

So we are redeemed, and the earth, he said, cradles them.

5.

The round sound of his words, boat's wheel turning, smoke
of his pipe vining our heads, pungent salted croakers,
bag of crab, soft-shells for frying—his left hand
slash with bone knife, deadman away, that

home-made mayonnaise laid on home-ovened bread, blessing
of crab and tomato leaking, hands growing pink,
tongue in my mouth, swallow and swallow,
sweet tea, buttered corn, and you,

my love, with your small sock of coins saved—how?—bought
berries, ice cream, even pie. From bean rows fireflies
stitching the last light, they coiled
like gold flecks in your hair first nights in our bedroom.

6.

Years pass. And homes we had. All we loved. I think of them
when I look up at the painting we hang, Frank Cole's tossed-out
portrait of tomatoes.

"Unfinishable!" The painter said. So, ours. *Tomatoes.*

Six feet by three feet, balloons in oil. I loved what I saw,
as I loved you, from the first, as the eye takes in the miracle
of birds thrown by wind at marsh grass. But in this, too,

I see the old man, shaved for death, laid out in her living room,
as was the custom, cheeks
pinked like what filled Frank's bowl, tomatoes

bursting in their last rest, swollen, the mind's passion. Mine.
Black shadows, and yellow streaks, and birthing green,
flesh blotched and blood-crests. How little I knew.

7.

In the painter's hand light sizzles and breathes. I see
life's bounty and gift. The love went row by row

where the red-winged birds hurled themselves at each turn
with the face of the woman who was wordless,
seeming to sing in that whistle-cry,
the salt-reeds like a violin layered and loosed, and she

at kitchen door called to him, as he recalled, eating with us.
His tractor's clatter easeful in empty long days. Almost enough.

8.

We have been married two years. I go to the base in my blue
Air Force uniform, the news is Vietnam, dead friends.

Then one day he appears, the old man, arms full of gifts.
Why fear death, he says, when there is so much to eat? I see

how we wake with small passions he taught us—we wanted
as they did, painter and planter, to stay alive. Fifty years

we'll be in love, ending, starting, days with food cooling,
plates clotted at sink, touches and angers, babies. Hunger.

When he left, his pipe-smoke hung in marsh air. Red wings
flashed like voices already forgotten. The marsh trembled,

his dead son from C130 off-loaded at Dover AFB. Salute.
Don't know, he said, what she sees in me. Maybe him.

In his hands *tomatoes, blood*. Then he would say, offering
fish or crabs, the bag of flesh, maybe you're hungry today?

9.

Hanging on our wall like a promise the painter's
tomatoes, six, secrets of creation. They bring
the blackbirds weaving sunsets like notes
a young musician might practice
until he has found his love. I see them land
on gold marsh reeds wind blows and keeps touching.
Such a glory of free spirit, defiant, ever undead.

They bring the man on his tractor, old then in his field
as I am now, his warted, sun-barnacled arms
full of the earth's taste, the dusky smell of Time.

In the flickering light of those days, death passed by us.
We ate, we made love, we laughed. What more
could we have asked? Taste them, he said,
his venerable voice at our door, that day, him looking up.